$9.95

ISBN-87793-432-0

AVE MARIA PRESS
Notre Dame, Indiana 46556

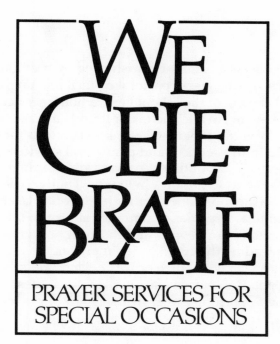

WE CELE-BRATE

PRAYER SERVICES FOR
SPECIAL OCCASIONS

WE CELEBRATE meets a common parish need by providing prayer services for special occasions—a pastoral council meeting, a parish picnic, the opening and closing of the school year, a home service for shut-ins—42 parish and home events in all. The major liturgical seasons can be celebrated fully through vesper services, special meals for families or school groups, scripture services and penitential services.

Provided here are the outlines, prayers and readings for highly adaptable services 10 to 15 minutes in length. They can be used as they are, or they can be the foundation for more elaborate celebrations; they can be individualized to a particular community or group; they can be led by one person or a number of people; and they can be adapted for use by clergy or laity in leading the community in prayer.

Drawn from the rich resource of *We Celebrate* and other missalettes from the J.S. Paluch Co. over the last two decades, these prayer services offer parishes the opportunity to grow in a spirit of prayer and worship as a community.

WE CELE-BRATE

PRAYER SERVICES FOR SPECIAL OCCASIONS

AVE MARIA PRESS
Notre Dame, Indiana 46556

Acknowledgments

These services previously appeared over two decades in the *Monthly Missalette, Seasonal Missalette,* and *We Celebrate Missalette* of the J.S. Paluch Company, thus fostering the preservation of ethnic traditions and encouraging a wider family devotional life in relation to the church's official liturgy.

The services in this book are not taken from an approved liturgical book. They are offered in the spirit of the *Constitution on the Liturgy,* no. 13, that non-liturgical devotions "harmonize with the liturgical seasons, accord with the sacred liturgy, are in some fashion derived from it, and lead the people to it."

The Reflective Prayer in "Our Daily Work: Penitential Service" taken from **This Week** vol.2, no. 40, Sept. 2, 1973. World Library Publications.

Excerpts from THE DOCUMENTS OF VATICAN II, Abbott-Gallagher edition, reprinted with permission of America Press, Inc., 106 West 56th Street, New York, NY 10019. © 1966 All Rights Reserved.

Scripture selections from **The New American Bible With Revised New Testament** Copyright © 1986 by the Confraternity of Christian Doctrine, Washington, DC, are all used with permission of the copyright owner. All rights reserved.

Apostolic Exhortation on Christian Joy (Pope Paul VI) and the encyclical *Pacem in Terris* (John XXIII) are available from the U.S. Catholic Conference, 3211 Fourth Street, NE, Washington, DC 20017-1194.

English translations of the *Magnificat, Nunc Dimittis, Te Deum* and Apostles' Creed: Copyright by the International Consultation on English Texts.

Poetic English translation of the Pentecost Sequence © 1964 United States Catholic Conference (formerly National Catholic Welfare Conference).

Material from the English translation of the Roman Missal, arrangement of responsorial psalms and antiphons from the Lectionary: Copyright © 1968, 1969, 1973, 1985 International Committee on English in the Liturgy, Inc. All rights reserved.

International Standard Book Number: 0-87793-432-0

Library of Congress Catalog Card Number: 90-82094

Cover and text design by Elizabeth J. French

Printed and bound in the United States of America.

Contents

Notes on Using This Book / 7

ADVENT AND CHRISTMAS / 9

Advent Vespers / 11
Advent Penitential Service / 15
Light in the Lord—Penitential Service / 18
A Festival of Lessons and Carols / 21
A Vigil Service Before Christmas / 23
Intercessions for Holy Family Day / 26
Scripture Service for Epiphany / 28

LENT AND HOLY WEEK / 31

Lenten Preparation—Home or School / 33
Lenten Vespers / 36
Lenten Meal—Home Service / 41
A Lenten Service Based on the Final Words of Christ / 43
Lent's Meaning—Penitential Service / 48
Now Is the Acceptable Time—Penitential Service / 52

EASTER AND PENTECOST / 57

Joy at Easter—Prayer Service / 59
Hope—Penitential Service / 62
Home Service for Pentecost / 65
Pentecost—Season for Renewal / 67
In the Spirit—Scripture Service / 71
Spirit of Joy—Prayer Service / 75
Jesus in Glory—Penitential Service / 78

PARISH CELEBRATIONS / 83

Service for the Opening of School / 85
Service to Close the School Year / 88
Prayers for a Parish Meeting / 91
Service for Travel / 93
Picnic Service / 95
Home Service for Shut-Ins / 98

Home Service—The Christian Family / 101
Prayer Service—Peace / 103
Service for Christian Unity / 107
Behold Your Mother—May Crowning Service / 110
The Gift of Beauty in the Land—Scripture Service / 115
Prayer Service Before Elections / 119
Independence Day Celebration / 122

PENITENTIAL SERVICES / 127

A New Beginning—Penitential Service / 129
Respect for Life—Penitential Service / 132
Heart for Hearts—Penitential Service / 136
Christian Joy—Penitential Service / 140
A Father's Love—Penitential Service / 144
Freedom—Penitential Service / 147
Our Daily Work—Penitential Service / 150
Our Call to Serve—Penitential Service / 153
Thanksgiving—Penitential Service / 155

Notes on Using This Book

The prayer services in this book are designed for a variety of uses. They can be used by school or religious education classes, families, or other groups within the parish. They offer those planning a prayer service the basic structure and key elements — introductory rites, a liturgy of the word, a resolution or blessing, and a concluding rite.

Planners can use the services as they appear or adapt them to suit the needs of the group. Most of the services can be led by either a priest or a lay person. The person leading the services might want to determine beforehand various postures for the service. In general, it is appropriate to stand during songs and prayers, to sit during the scripture readings, homilies and reflections, and to kneel during penitential prayers.

The texts for the readings from scripture do not appear in the book unless they have been adapted in some way. The person planning the service will need to find these readings in the Bible or Lectionary and make them available to the person doing the readings. The lectionary number for many of the selections appears in parentheses after the citation.

Suggested songs are given for the opening and closing of each service. These can be found in many parish hymnals or worship aids. Other music that a particular group may be more familiar with may be substituted.

Responses by the congregation may be duplicated for a one-time use by participants.

ADVENT
AND
CHRISTMAS

ADVENT VESPERS

The appropriate number of candles are lighted on the Advent wreath. After the entrance procession the minister may incense it.

Opening Song: **The King of Glory; O Come, O Come Emmanuel** or any suitable song.

Thanksgiving

Minister: Let us give thanks to the Lord our God.

All: **It is right to give him thanks and praise.**

Minister: Father, all powerful and everliving God, . . .

    Week 1—Preface 31 (Sundays III)
    Week 2—Preface 35 (Sundays VIII) or Preface 42 (Weekdays VI)
    Week 3—Preface 83 (Independence Day)
    Week 4—Preface 44 (Annunciation)

The minister omits the preface's final sentence, supplanting it with:

And so we offer you our praise this afternoon/evening, through Christ our Lord.

All: Amen.

Psalms

Select two psalms from the following.

Psalm 90:3-4, 5-6, 12-13, 14 and 17 (L130-C)

    R. O Lord, you have been our refuge through all generations.

Psalm 131:1, 2, 3 (L152-A)

    R. My soul is longing for your peace.

Seasonal psalm: Select an appropriate responsorial psalm from one of the Sunday liturgies.

New Testament Canticle

Sion, Sing, Break Into Song, Lucien Deiss, C.S.Sp.

Reading

Incensation of the word of God may precede its proclamation. On special days, a second reading may follow. It may be scriptural or contemporary. Other readings are available in the Lectionary *and* Christian Prayer: Liturgy of the Hours.

Week 1—Isaiah 65:17-21 (L245)

Week 2—Isaiah 49:8-15 (L247)

Week 3—Isaiah 42:1-7 (L258)

Week 4—Isaiah 26:7-9, 12, 16-19 (L392)

Silent reflection or a brief homily follows.

Gospel Canticle

1. *The Magnificat (Lk 1:46-55) is appropriate for use in the late afternoon or early evening. It may be sung in a musical version such as* **Our Lady's Song of Praise** *or* **Canticle of Mary**, *chanted or recited.*

**My soul proclaims the greatness of the Lord,
my spirit rejoices in God my Savior
for he has looked with favor on his lowly servant.**

**From this day all generations will call me blessed:
the Almighty has done great things for me,
and holy is his Name.**

**He has mercy on those who fear him
in every generation.**

**He has shown the strength of his arm,
he has scattered the proud in their conceit.
He has cast down the mighty from their thrones,
and has lifted up the lowly.**

**He has filled the hungry with good things,
and the rich he has sent away empty.
He has come to the help of his servant Israel**

for he has remembered his promise of mercy,
the promise he made to our fathers,
to Abraham and his children forever.

Glory to the Father, . . .

2.   *The Nunc Dimittis (Lk 2:29-32) is appropriate for use late in the evening. It may be chanted or recited as follows.*

Lord, now you let your servant go in peace;
your word has been fulfilled:
my own eyes have seen the salvation
which you have prepared in the sight of every people:
a light to reveal you to the nations
and the glory of your people Israel.

Glory to the Father, . . .

Intercessions

Selections appear in Christian Prayer: Liturgy of the Hours *and also in the* Sacramentary, *Appendix 1, nos. 1, 2 and 3.*

Concluding Prayer

Minister: Let us conclude our prayer with the words of Jesus:

All: **Our Father, . . .**

Minister: When evening comes, Lord, we pray.

We praise and bless you
for the joy of those who love one another,
for the efforts of those who work,
for the patience of those who suffer.
We ask pardon of you
for the weakness of our love
on the road that leads to you.
Lead us beyond the night
to the dawn of eternal day
when we will see you face to face.

We ask this through Christ our Lord.

All: **Amen.**

All may exchange a farewell greeting of peace.

Dismissal

Minister: Bow your heads and pray for God's blessing. May God the Father and the Lord Jesus grant peace and love and faith to us all.

All: **Amen.**

Minister: Grace be with all who love our Lord Jesus Christ with unfailing love.

All: **Amen.**

A priest or deacon adds:

> May almighty God bless you,
> the Father, and the Son and the Holy Spirit.

All: **Amen.**

Closing song: **Day Is Done** or any suitable song.

Advent Penitential Service

Introductory Rites

Opening Song: **Come O Long Awaited Savior** or any suitable song.

Call to Worship

Minister: Seek the LORD while he may be found,
　　　　　　call to him while he is near.　　　　　　　　　Is 55:6

All: **Let [us] turn to the LORD for mercy,**
　　　　to our God, who is generous in forgiving.　　　Is 55:7

Opening Prayer

Minister: You were foretold by the prophets:
　　　　　　Lord have mercy.　　　　　　　**Lord have mercy.**

　　　　　　You came to save us from sin:
　　　　　　Christ have mercy.　　　　　　**Christ have mercy.**

　　　　　　You are the Light who scatters the darkness of sin:
　　　　　　Lord have mercy.　　　　　　　**Lord have mercy.**

Minister: Let us pray.

　　　　　　God of all ages,
　　　　　　your only Son became flesh
　　　　　　to free us from the bondage of sin.
　　　　　　Help us now to cleanse our souls
　　　　　　and to prepare room in our hearts,
　　　　　　that we may be ready to meet him when he comes.

　　　　　　We ask this through Christ our Lord.

All: **Amen.**

Reading of the Word of God

First Reading: 1 John 1:5 — 2:2 (L698)
　　　　[Forgiveness follows acknowledgment of our sin.]

Response: Psalm 25:8-11

All: **Good and upright is the LORD;**
           thus he shows sinners the way.
       He guides the humble to justice,
           he teaches the humble his way.
       All the paths of the LORD are kindness and constancy
           toward those who keep his covenant and his decrees.
       For your name's sake, O LORD,
           you will pardon my guilt, great as it is.

Gospel: John 3:16-21 (L756-10)
     [Forgiveness comes through Jesus.]

Response: **The Advent of Our God** or any suitable song.

Homily

Resolution

(Psalm 51:3-19)

Minister: Have mercy on me, O God, in your goodness;
           in the greatness of your compassion wipe out my offense.
       Thorougly wash me from my guilt
           and of my sin cleanse me.

All: **For I acknowledge my offense,**
           and my sin is before me always:
       "Against you only have I sinned,
           and done what is evil in your sight" —
       That you may be justified in your sentence,
           vindicated when you condemn.

Minister: Indeed, in guilt was I born,
           and in sin my mother conceived me.
       Behold, you are pleased with sincerity of heart
           and in my inmost being you teach me wisdom.

All: **Cleanse me of sin with hyssop, that I may be purified;**
           wash me, and I shall be whiter than snow.
       Let me hear the sounds of joy and gladness;
           the bones you have crushed shall rejoice.
       Turn away your face from my sins,
           and blot out all my guilt.

Minister: A clean heart create for me, O God,
    and a steadfast spirit renew within me.
Cast me not out from your presence,
    and your holy spirit take not from me.
Give me back the joy of your salvation,
    and a willing spirit sustain in me.

All: **I will teach transgressors your ways,
    and sinners shall return to you.
Free me from blood guilt, O God, my saving God;
    then my tongue shall revel in your justice.**

Minister: O LORD, open my lips,
    and my mouth shall proclaim your praise.
For you are not pleased with sacrifices;
    should I offer a holocaust, you would not accept it.

All: **My sacrifice, O God, is a contrite spirit;
    a heart contrite and humbled, O God, you will not spurn.**

Concluding Rite

Dismissal

Minister: Go in peace
and may Jesus the Light shine on your paths
and in your heart forever.

All: **Thanks be to God.**

Closing Song: **People Look East** or any suitable song.

Light in the Lord—
Penitential Service

The church is dimly lighted. All receive unlighted candles on arrival.

Introductory Rites

Opening Song: **Jesus the New Covenant** or any suitable song.

Call to Worship

Minister: The night is advanced, the day is at hand. Let us then throw off the works of darkness [and] put on the armor of light.

Rom 13:12

All: **[We] are children of light and children of the day.**
We are not of the night or of darkness.   1 Thes 5:5

Reading of the Word of God

First Reading: Isaiah 59:1-4; 7-8

[We separate ourselves from God through our sins.]

Afterward we pause to reflect on our lives, how by sin the kingdom of light has been frustrated.

Second Reading: Isaiah 59:9-12

[We acknowledge our sinfulness.]

The people's candles are lighted after the reading.

Third Reading: Isaiah 9:1-3

[The Lord brings joy to his people.]

Response: John 9:4-5

All: **We do the works of the one who sent [us] while it is day.**
Night is coming when no one can work.
While [we are] in the world, [we] are the light of the world.

All the lights are turned on.

Song: **We Are the Light of the World** or any suitable song.

Fourth Reading: Ephesians 5:8-14 (L31-A)
   [We are light in the Lord Jesus Christ.]

Response: **O Lord of Light** or any suitable song.

All extinguish their candles.

Homily

Act of Contrition

Minister: Let us acknowledge our sins before God.

All: **My God,**
I am sorry for my sins with all my heart.
In choosing to do wrong
and failing to do good,
I have sinned against you
whom I should love above all things.
I firmly intend, with your help,
to do penance,
to sin no more,
and to avoid whatever leads me to sin.
Our Savior Jesus Christ
suffered and died for us.
In his name, my God, have mercy.

Resolution

Minister: If we walk in light, as [God] is in the light,
   then we have fellowship with one another,
   and the blood of his Son Jesus cleanses us from all sin.   1 Jn 1:7

All: **He delivered us from the power of darkness**
and transferred us to the kingdom of his beloved Son,
in whom we have redemption, the forgiveness of sins.

Col 1:13-14

Minister: We proclaim our faith in the Light of the world:

All: **God so loved the world that he gave his only Son,**
so that everyone who believes in him might not perish
but might have eternal life.
For God did not send his Son into the world
to condemn the world,
but that the world might be saved through him.
Whoever believes in him will not be condemned,
but whoever does not believe has already been condemned,
because he has not believed in the name of the only Son of
God.
And this is the verdict,
that the light came into the world,
but people preferred darkness to light,
because their works were evil.
For everyone who does wicked things hates the light
and does not come toward the light,
so that his works might not be exposed.
But whoever lives the truth comes to the light,
so that his works may be clearly seen as done in God.

Jn 3:16-21

Minister: While you have the light, believe in the light,
so that you may become children of the light.   Jn 12:36

All: **The light shines in the darkness,**
and the darkness has not overcome it.   Jn 1:5

Concluding Rite

Dismissal

Minister: Go in peace.

All: **Thanks be to God.**

Closing song: **O Come, O Come, Emmanuel** or any suitable song.

A Festival of Lessons and Carols

Archbishop Benson of Truro in England based this service on the monastic tradition of reading nine lessons with sung responses as part of the matins on Christmas Day. The service has been sung in King's College Chapel, Cambridge, on Christmas Eve for nearly 50 years.

The suggested carols are available in Book 1 of *Carols for Choirs*, Oxford University Press, and in the *Oxford Book of Carols*. The congregation can join the choir with the carols found in the parish hymnal or worship aid.

This service might be held on the third Sunday of Advent or any of the Sundays in Advent. The service can be shortened or rearranged to suit the particular community.

Organ Prelude

Candlelight Procession: **Once in Royal David's City; O Come, O Come, Emmanuel**.

Opening Prayer: The minister introduces the themes and says an appropriate prayer.

The lessons follow. Each passage is read by a different member of the community.

The First Lesson: Genesis 3:9-15 (L90-B)

God announces in the garden of Eden that the seed of woman shall bruise the serpent's head.

Carol: **Adam Lay Ibounden; Lo! How a Rose E'er Blooming**

The Second Lesson: Genesis 22:15-18 (L26-B)

God promises to faithful Abraham that in his seed shall all nations of the earth be blessed.

Carol: **Tomorrow Shall Be My Dancing Day; Behold a Virgin Bearing Him**

The Third Lesson: Isaiah 9:2-7 (L14)

Christ's birth and kingdom are foretold by Isaiah.

Carol: **Ding, Dong, Merrily on High; On Jordan's Bank**

The Fourth Lesson: Micah 5:2-5a (L12-C)

The prophet Micah foretells the glory of little Bethlehem.

Carol: **There Is No Rose; O Little Town of Bethlehem**

The Fifth Lesson: Luke 1:26-38 (L11-B)
  The angel Gabriel salutes the Blessed Virgin Mary.

Carol: **Blessed Be That Maid Mary; What Child Is This?**

The Sixth Lesson: Matthew 1:18-24 (L10-A) or Luke 2:1, 3-7
  St. Matthew (St. Luke) tells of the birth of Jesus.

Carol: **Sussex Carol; God Rest You Merry; Silent Night**

The Seventh Lesson: Luke 2:8-16
  The shepherds go to the manger.

Carol: **Infant Holy, Infant Lowly; Gesu Bambino; Joy to the World**

The Eighth Lesson: Matthew 2:1-12 (L20)
  The wise men are led by the star to Jesus.

Carol: **Away in a Manger; O Come All Ye Faithful; We Three Kings**

The Ninth Lesson: John 1:1-14 (L16, partial)
  St. John unfolds the great mystery of the Incarnation.

Closing Song: **Hark! The Herald Angels Sing**

A Vigil Service Before Christmas

This service can suitably close the Advent season. It may not be joined to the Mass. Each part may also be used separately.

1. The Great "O" antiphons

Opening Song: **Lo, How a Rose E'er Blooming** or **People Look East** or any suitable song.

Commentator: During these past weeks we have been preparing to celebrate the Lord's coming. Today we know that he will come and in the morning we will see his glory. Now we recall the long centuries during which humanity longed for salvation. We relive that expectation as we sing an ancient Advent song.

The church lights are subdued. An unlighted seven-branch candelabrum stands in a central location. One candle is lighted during the introduction to each verse of the song, beginning with the lowest candle on each side of the candelabrum. Thus the top candle is the last lighted. Scripture references provide the development of these introductions or may be used as readings if desired.

Commentator: Jesus is our Emmanuel, "God with us," promised when our first parents became exiles from God and captives of sin. Because we desire him among us, we sing: "O come, O come, Emmanuel!"   Is 7:14

Song: **O Come, O Come, Emmanuel**, verse 1

Commentator: Jesus is the Word of God and Wisdom of the Father for all eternity. We sing the praises of him who existed before the world began: "Come, O Wisdom!"   Sir 24, Wis 8

Song: **O Come, O Come, Emmanuel**, verse 2

Commentator: The Lord of might appeared amid flames of the burning bush on Mount Sinai. We ask him to make us worthy to enter the Promised Land. We call to him: "Come, O Lord of might."   Ex 3

Song: **O Come, O Come, Emmanuel**, verse 3

Commentator: Jesus is the Flower of Jesse's root. No greater flower bloomed on the family tree of Jesse, King David's father. Jesus would become the tree of life that brings us salvation, and so we pray: "Come, O Rod of Jesse's stem!" Is 11

Song: **O Come, O Come, Emmanuel**, verse 4

Commentator: Jesus is the key of David. He came to unlock the prison of death and release us from the bonds of sin. We are grateful that he gave us freedom as we sing: "Come, O Key of David!" Is 22

Song: **O Come, O Come, Emmanuel**, verse 5

Commentator: Jesus is the Daystar, the sun that brightens the world's darkness. We will see him in splendor when he comes again. On that day he will cheer us, and so we sing: "Come, O Daystar!" Ps 107:10-16; Is 9:1-6

Song: **O Come, O Come, Emmanuel**, verse 6

Commentator: Jesus is the Desired One of the nations, who unites us into one family. He was foretold as King and Prince of Peace. We his people sing: "O Come, Desire of Nations!" Is 26

Song: **O Come, O Come, Emmanuel**, verse 7

A choral/congregational program of carols may follow, and the service may conclude with the posada *procession.*

2. The *Posada* Procession

The crib scene has been prepared without the figures of Jesus, Mary and Joseph. It is now illuminated. The following ceremony is based on the Hispanic custom of the posada (inn) *procession searching for a place of shelter and rest.*

Commentator: During these past weeks we have been preparing to celebrate the Lord's coming. Today we know that he will come and in the morning we shall see his glory.

Song: **O Little Town of Bethlehem**, verse 1.

The presiding minister and other ministers go in procession to a side entrance of the church. After the first verse there is silence, and a knock is sounded at that door. A person there may engage in this dialogue with the people.

Joseph: In the name of heaven, good friends, give us a place to stay this night.

All: **This is not an inn; keep going. We don't open to strangers.**

During the song's second verse, the procession moves to another side entrance. The knocking occurs again, followed by this dialogue.

Joseph: I am Joseph, the carpenter from Nazareth. Do not refuse us, that God may reward you.

All: **We don't care who you are; let us sleep. We already told you we won't let you in.**

During the third verse, the procession moves to the main entrance. The knocking occurs again, followed by this dialogue.

Joseph: My beloved wife Mary can go no farther. She is heaven's Queen who will bear God's Son.

All: **Enter holy pilgrims; you may use this poor place. Our houses and our hearts are open to you.**

The presiding minister opens the door to admit Mary and Joseph. During the singing of the fourth verse, representatives of parish organizations or children accompany the procession to the crib scene, carrying the figures of Jesus, Mary and Joseph for placement there.

Commentator: As the procession bears the figures of Jesus, Mary and Joseph to the crib, we sing a song that expresses the gathering of all of us in worship.

Song: **Silent Night** or **O Come, Little Children** or any suitable song.

The Christmas crib may be blessed at this time.

Intercessions for Holy Family Day

The terms "family" and "household" have broadened in meaning beyond the usual intimate sense of spouses and children. The following intercessions may be recited by families or other groups as a reminder that there are also one-parent families, blended families, individuals living alone, the parish family, the community, the nation, the family of nations and the household of faith. *These intercessions may not be used as part of the eucharistic liturgy.*

Reader: We pray for the household of the faith, the church, charged with the task of proclaiming the word.

All: **Lord, may we all, members and ministers, be faithful to our baptismal dignity and responsibilities.**

Reader: We pray for our nation and the family of nations, facing serious ethical and moral, social and economic judgments.

All: **Lord, guide those who lead us in their concern for justice, charity and peace.**

Reader: We pray for all married couples, who have pledged to be faithful to each other.

All: **Lord, may the fervor of their love show to the world your regard and care for the church.**

Reader: We pray for all parents, parents without partners, the married and single, widowed, separated and divorced.

All: **Lord, help them to share their faith and show their trust as they listen to, affirm and support their children.**

Reader: We pray for infants and children, especially the abused and those without parents.

All: **Lord, let them know your love through the tenderness of all who care for them.**

Reader: We pray for all young men and women as they approach life's decisions.

All: **Lord, give them a full and happy youth, and open their hearts to your world's goodness and beauty.**

Reader: We pray for all who are single by choice or circumstance, living in the workaday world.

All: **Lord, may their lives of generous service to others bring them the reward of deep friendships.**

Reader: We pray for all who are celibate for the sake of your reign.

All: **Lord, support them in the joy of their vocations, that their lives may manifest the reign of God.**

Reader: We pray for all who have no family or home.

All: **Lord, show the gentleness of your presence to those who are alone and have no hope but you.**

Reader: We pray for all in the autumn of life with its prospects of loneliness and diminished health.

All: **Lord, grant them a secure and serene old age, and guide their steps on the road of peace.**

Reader: We pray for all who have lost a spouse or child.

All: **Lord, let your compassion heal their hearts.**

Reader: We pray for all our beloved dead, especially ——.

All: **Eternal rest grant unto them, O Lord, and let perpetual light shine upon them.**

Reader: Gracious God,
give us all a share of joy and happiness,
that we may constantly discover your love
and praise and glorify you in our daily lives.
May we arrive at the perfect joy,
which is to live with you, your Son and the Holy
Spirit, forever and ever.

All: Amen.

Scripture Service for Epiphany

The solemnity of Epiphany marks the arrival in Bethlehem of the astrologers from the East. As representatives of the world outside Judaism, their visit signifies the manifestation of Jesus to the Gentiles. Since their discovery of him who was later to call himself the Light of the world was by means of a great light in the sky, Epiphany has come to be associated with the theme of light. This service traces the motif of light through the Hebrew and Christian scriptures.

Introductory Rites

Opening Song: **The First Noel** or **What Child Is This?**, especially verse 3 of either, or any suitable song.

Opening Prayer

Minister: Let us pray.

O God,
when you began your wonderful work of creation,
you chose first to create light.
But humanity resisted your truth,
and chose instead to walk in interior darkness.
In your goodness you chose to rekindle a light
in the person of your own Son.
To the Father who created light,
to the Son who is our light,
and to the Holy Spirit who enlightens all
be glory and honor forever and ever.

All: **Amen.**

Reading of the Word of God

First Reading: Exodus 13:17-18,21-22
[The light of God leads the Israelites to freedom.]

Response: Isaiah 60:1-6 (L20)

All: **Rise up in splendor! Your light has come,
the glory of the Lord shines upon you.**

See, darkness covers the earth,
    and thick clouds cover the peoples;
But upon you the LORD shines,
    and over you appears his glory.
Nations shall walk by your light,
    and kings by your shining radiance.
Raise your eyes and look about;
    they all gather and come to you:
Your sons come from afar,
    and your daughters in the arms of their nurses.
Then you shall be radiant at what you see,
    your heart shall throb and overflow,
For the riches of the sea shall be emptied out before you,
    the wealth of nations shall be brought to you.
Caravans of camels shall fill you,
    dromedaries from Midian and Ephah;
All from Sheba shall come
    bearing gold and frankincense,
    and proclaiming the praises of the LORD.

Second Reading: Ephesians 5:8-14 (L31-A)

[Paul tells us we are children of light.]

Response: 1 John 1:5-7

All: **Now this is the message that we have heard from him and proclaim to you: God is light, and in him there is no darkness at all. If we say, "We have fellowship with him," while we continue to walk in darkness, we lie and do not act in truth. But if we walk in the light as he is in the light, then we have fellowship with one another, and the blood of his Son Jesus cleanses us from all sin.**

Gospel: Matthew 2:1-12 (L20)

[Magi from the east follow the star to Jesus.]

Response: **We Three Kings** or **A Child Is Born**, verses 5 and 6, or **Songs of Thankfulness and Praise**, verse 1, or any suitable song.

Homily

Prayer

Minister: Lord Jesus Christ, you are the Light of our world,
the true light, which enlightens everyone.   Jn 1:9

All: **The light shines in the darkness,**
and the darkness has not overcome it.   Jn 1:5

Minister: Whoever walks in the dark does not know where he is going.
     Jn 12:35

All: **He delivered us from the power of darkness**
and transferred us to the kingdom of his beloved Son.
     Col 1:13

Minister: Now, Master, you may let your servant go
in peace according to your word,   Lk 2:29

All: **for my eyes have seen your salvation,**
which you prepared in the sight of all the peoples,
a light for revelation to the Gentiles,
and glory for your people Israel.   Lk 2:30-32

Concluding Rite

Blessing

Minister: Now to him who can strengthen you, according to [the] gospel
and the proclamation of Jesus Christ, according to the
revelation of the mystery kept secret for long ages but now
manifested through the prophetic writings and, according to
the command of the eternal God, made known to all nations to
bring about the obedience of faith,

All: **to the only wise God,**
through Jesus Christ be glory
forever and ever. Amen.   Rom 16:25-27

Closing Song: **What Star Is This?**, verse 2, **As With Gladness**; **Joy to the World**
or any suitable song.

LENT
AND
HOLY WEEK

LENTEN PREPARATION—
HOME OR SCHOOL

The minister for this service may be a priest, deacon or lay person.

Introductory Rites

Opening Song: **Giver of the Perfect Gift** or any suitable song.

Call to Celebration

Minister: Help us, O God our savior.
Because of the glory of your name.

All: **Deliver us and pardon our sins
for your name's sake.**

Opening Prayer

Minister: Let us pray.

Father, we come to learn the meaning of Lent.
Help us choose the way of penance
which will lead to the fulfillment of our baptismal promises.

All: **Amen.**

Reading of the Word of God

First Reading: Deuteronomy 9:25-27
[Moses prays for forty days.]

Response: **From the Depths** or any suitable song.

Gospel: Mark 1:12-15 (L23-B)
[Jesus calls us to fulfill our promises.]

Discussion

A. Prayer:

Will we attend daily Mass, the Way of the Cross or other services suggested in the parish bulletin? Will we pray together in the family or classroom? Do we each have a personal prayer life?

Especially with children, pretzels can be used frequently during Lent as a reminder of prayer. The pretzel originated in the fifth century as a Lenten bread. In the ancient Lenten fast, milk, butter, cheese, eggs, cream and meat were prohibited. As a result, small breads were made of flour, water and salt. They were shaped in the form of arms crossed in prayer depicting the ancient practice of praying with the arms crossed. The breads were called "little arms" (bracellae). This Latin word is the origin of the German word "pretzel" (brezel).

B. Penance:

Will we by-pass amusements, do without treats, keep an alms box?

The funds saved as a result of sacrifice can be designated for a cause the family or class chooses.

C. Charity:

Will we practice the corporal works of mercy: feed the hungry, give drink to the thirsty, shelter the homeless, clothe the naked, visit the sick and imprisoned and be helpful at home and in school?

The Lenten Overseas Aid Collection will provide an opportunity for our practical charity.

Procession

The children may carry a cross in procession and place it in a prominent location in the home or classroom as a reminder of their Lenten intentions. It may have before it a basket with their Lenten practices written on slips of paper.

Minister: We adore you, O Christ, and we praise you.

All: **Because by your holy cross you have redeemed the world.**

Minister:	Let us pray.
	God, our Father, we honor the cross of Jesus. During Lent may it remind us of the suffering of your Son. Let it recall to us the promises we have made and help us to keep them.
	Grant that the cross may comfort us, protect us and shield us from all evil.
	We ask this through Christ our Lord.
All:	**Amen.**

Conclusion

Minister:	For our forgetfulness:	**Forgive us, Lord.**
	For our unkindness to one another:	**Forgive us, Lord.**
	For our selfishness or refusal to help:	**Forgive us, Lord.**
	For our broken promises:	**Forgive us, Lord.**
	For our failure to do good:	**Forgive us, Lord.**
	For our secret sins:	**Forgive us, Lord.**

Other petitions may be added.

Minister:	Lord, let your face shine upon us.
All:	**Look upon us kindly and give us peace.**

Closing Song: **Make Us True Servants** or any suitable song.

Lenten Vespers

The general theme for these weeks is a journey: to Jerusalem, to Holy Week and to Easter, following the general pattern of the Lenten Sunday themes.

Week 1:   The desert

Week 2:   The mountain

Week 3:   Life-giving water

Week 4:   The warmth of God's light

Week 5:   Natural and spiritual growth

Week 6:   Jerusalem

Introduction

Good Friday's acclamation is sung, once or three times, as all face the processional cross. Incensation of the cross accompanies the singing.

Minister: This is the wood of the cross,
on which hung the Savior of the world.

All: **Come, let us worship.**

Evening Hymn

Select one of the following or any suitable song.

Week 1:   **These Forty Days of Lent**

Week 2:   **God's Holy Mountain We Ascend**

Week 3:   **Born Again**

Week 4:   **God, Full of Mercy**

Week 5:   **Grant to Us, O Lord**

Week 6:   **All Glory, Laud and Honor**

Thanksgiving

Minister: Let us give thanks to the Lord our God.

All: **It is right to give him thanks and praise.**

Minister: Father, all-powerful and ever-living God, . . .

>   Week 1—Preface 35 (Sundays VII) or Preface 9 (Lent II)
>   Week 2—Preface 50 (Transfiguration)
>   Week 3—Preface 30 (Sundays II)
>   Week 4—Preface 29 (Sundays I)
>   Week 5—Preface 33 (Sundays V) or Preface 84 (Thanksgiving)
>   Week 6—Preface 18 (Passion II) or Preface 46 (Triumph of the Cross)

The minister omits the preface's final sentence, supplanting it with:

>   And so we offer you our praise this afternoon/evening, through
>   Christ our Lord.

All: **Amen.**

Psalms

Select two psalms from those suggested.

1

Psalm 130:1-2, 3-4, 4-6, 7-8 (L34-A)

>   **R.   With the Lord there is mercy, and fullness of redemption.**

Psalm 131:1, 2, 3 (L152-A)

>   **R.   My soul is longing for your peace.**

2

Psalm 46:1-2, 4-5, 7-8 (L246)

>   **R.   God is our refuge and our strength.**

Psalm 90:3-4, 5-6, 12-13, 14 and 17 (L130-C)

>   **R.   O Lord, you have been our refuge through all generations.**

3

Seasonal Psalm: Select an appropriate responsorial psalm from one of the
>   Sunday liturgies.

New Testament Canticle

Select one of the following:

> **Keep in Mind**, Lucien Deiss, C.S.Sp.
> **Priestly People**, Lucien Deiss, C.S.Sp.

Reading

Incensation of the word of God may precede its proclamation. On special days, a second reading may follow. It may be scriptural or contemporary, for example, from the bishop's Lenten pastoral letter. Other readings are available in the Lectionary *and* Christian Prayer: Liturgy of the Hours.

> Week 1—Hebrews 3:7-14 (L308) or Ezekiel 20:13-17
> Week 2—Hebrews 12:18-19, 21-24 (L326)
> Week 3—Isaiah 55:1-11 (L42-5)
> Week 4—2 Corinthians 4:5-18
> Week 5—Hebrews 6:1-8
> Week 6—Zechariah 12:10-11 (L97-C) or Zechariah 9:9-10 (L836-3)

Silent reflection or a brief homily follows.

Gospel Canticle

During the canticle incense may be used.

1

The Magnificat (Lk 1:46-55) is appropriate for use in the late afternoon or early evening. It may be sung in a musical version such as **Our Lady's Song of Praise** *or* **Canticle of Mary**, *chanted or recited.*

**My soul proclaims the greatness of the Lord,
my spirit rejoices in God my Savior
for he has looked with favor on his lowly servant.**

**From this day all generations will call me blessed:
the Almighty has done great things for me,
and holy is his Name.**

**He has mercy on those who fear him
in every generation.**

He has shown the strength of his arm,

he has scattered the proud in their conceit.
He has cast down the mighty from their thrones,
and has lifted up the lowly.

He has filled the hungry with good things,
and the rich he has sent away empty.
He has come to the help of his servant Israel
for he has remembered his promise of mercy,
the promise he made to our fathers,
to Abraham and his children forever.

Glory to the Father, . . .

2

The Nunc Dimittis (Lk 2:29-32) is appropriate for use late in the evening. It may be chanted or recited.

Lord, now you let your servant go in peace;
your word has been fulfilled:
my own eyes have seen the salvation
which you have prepared in the sight of every people:
a light to reveal you to the nations
and the glory of your people Israel.

Glory to the Father, . . .

Intercessions

Selections appear in Christian Prayer: Liturgy of the Hours *and also in the* Sacramentary, *Appendix 1, nos. 1, 2 and 6.*

Minister: Let us conclude our prayer with the words of Jesus.

All: **Our Father, . . .**

Concluding Prayer

Minister: As our day ends, Lord,
may we take our rest in you.
Let your holy angels watch over us.
Then bring us to the light of another day,
as a promise of our sharing in your resurrection.

May each future day be spent in your service,
until we enter into the joy of your presence.
Stay with us, Lord, this night and all our days.

We ask this in your holy name.

All: **Amen.**

All may exchange a greeting of peace.

Dismissal

Minister: Bow your heads and pray for God's blessing.

Blest be God,
who gives salvation through our Lord Jesus Christ.

All: **Amen.**

Minister: He died and rose again for us
so that, awake or asleep,
we might live together with him.

All: **Amen.**

A priest or deacon adds:

May almighty God bless you,
the Father, and the Son, and the Holy Spirit.

All: **Amen.**

Lenten Meal— Home Service

The table is prepared with candles and simple Lenten foods in imitation of the Seder table at Passover time: salad, hard-boiled eggs, bread and drink.

Blessing

To symbolize God's presence, the hostess lights the candles while saying:

Hostess: Blessed be the LORD, the God of [creation,]
            who alone does wondrous deeds.

All: **And blessed forever be his glorious name;**
          may the whole earth be filled with his glory.

Ps 72:18-19

The host lifts his drink-filled cup and says:

Host: Blessed day by day be the LORD,
        who bears our burdens; God, who is our salvation.

Ps 68:20

All: [Our] help is from the Lord
        who made heaven and earth.

Ps 121:2

All drink from their cups.

First Reading: Deuteronomy 26:16-19 (L230)
    [Covenant People]

Response: **These Forty Days of Lent** or any suitable song.

Lenten Meal

As the song ends, the host passes around the salad, eggs, bread and drink. Conversation may be directed to topics of Lenten renewal or to everyday opportunities for Christian witness. When the eating ends, the cups are filled again.

Gospel: Mark 12:28-34 (L153-B)
    [The Greatest Commandment]

Intercessions

Leader: God our Father, you have gathered us around this table. Let the words of the covenant shake us out of our easy ways, that we may repent and take positive steps in our witness to you.

Reader: That Lent may bring a return to the covenant in which we love God and our neighbor as Jesus teaches, we pray to the Lord.

R.   Lord, renew the face of the earth.

That Lent may be a time for truth, justice and peace in the decisions of state, national and world governments, we pray to the Lord.   **R.**

That Lent may be a time for positive efforts toward renewal of our covenant promises to love, we pray to the Lord.   **R.**

That Lent may provide each family with time to strengthen bonds of love and communication, we pray to the Lord.   **R.**

That Lent's prayers and sacrifices may bring relief to those suffering from any need, we pray to the Lord.   **R.**

We may add other personal intentions, concluding each with the response.

Leader: These are our prayers.
We join to them our promise to live Jesus' way of love.
We seal this prayer and promise with this last cup.

All drink from their cups.

Song: **Priestly People** or any suitable song.

Conclusion

Dessert may now be shared as we draw the conversation to a close.

A Lenten Service Based on the Final Words of Christ

Posters, banners and slides may serve as "stations." These may be especially meaningful to children if they prepare the stations themselves and adapt the service to their own understanding.

Introductory Rites

Opening Song: **Were You There?** or any suitable song.

Call to Celebration

Minister: Draw near to God, and he will draw near to you.

Jas 4:8

All: **Hear, O God, [our] cry; listen to [our] prayer!**

Ps 61:2

Opening Prayer

Minister: Let us pray.

Lord Jesus Christ, our Redeemer,
we confidently gather about your cross.
We ask mercy for ourselves and all those for whom we pray.
Grant us the light and strength to know you and love you, to
be sorry for our sins and serve you in one another.

We ask this in your holy name.

All: **Amen.**

Reading of the Word of God

I

Luke 23:32-34

Narrator: Now two others, both criminals, were led away with [Jesus] to
be crucified. When they came to the place called Skull, they
crucified him and the criminals there, one on his right, the
other on his left. [Then Jesus said:

All: **"Father, forgive them for they know not what they do."**]

Silent prayer or meditative comment or prepared prayer may follow.

Minister: Have mercy on us, O Lord.

All: **Jesus, we believe in you, we hope in you, we love you. Through your cross you brought us the hope of resurrection.**

Song: **Where Charity and Love Prevail**, verses 3-4.

II

Luke 23:39-43

Narrator: Now one of the criminals hanging there reviled Jesus, saying:

Speaker: "Are you not the Messiah? Save yourself and us."

Narrator: The other, however, rebuking him, said in reply:

Speaker: "Have you no fear of God, for you are subject to the same condemnation? And indeed, we have been condemned justly, for the sentence we received corresponds to our crimes, but this man has done nothing criminal."

Narrator: Then he said,

Speaker: "Jesus, remember me when you come into your kingdom."

Narrator: [Jesus] replied to him,

All: **"Amen, I say to you, today you will be with me in Paradise."**

Silent prayer or meditative comment or prepared prayer may follow.

Minister: Have mercy on us, O Lord.

All: **Jesus, we believe in you, we hope in you, we love you. Through your cross you brought us the hope of resurrection.**

Song: **Keep in Mind**, verses 4-6.

III

John 19:25-27

Narrator: Standing by the cross of Jesus were his mother, his mother's sister, Mary the wife of Clopas, and Mary of Magdala. When Jesus saw his mother and the disciple there whom he loved, he said to his mother,

All:	"**Woman, behold your son.**"
Narrator:	Then he said to the disciple,
All:	"**Behold, your mother.**"

Silent prayer or meditative comment or prepared prayer may follow.

Minister:	Have mercy on us, O Lord.
All:	**Jesus, we believe in you, we hope in you, we love you.** **Through your cross you brought us the hope of resurrection.**
Song:	**Sing of Mary**, verse 3.

IV

Matthew 27:45-46

Narrator:	From noon onward, darkness came over the whole land until three in the afternoon. And about three o'clock, Jesus cried out in a loud voice,
All:	"**My God, my God, why have you forsaken me?**"

Silent prayer or meditative comment or prepared prayer may follow.

Minister:	Have mercy on us, O Lord.
All:	**Jesus, we believe in you, we hope in you, we love you.** **Through your cross you brought us the hope of resurrection.**
Song:	**From the Depths**, verses 1-2.

V

John 19:28

Narrator:	Aware that everything was now finished, in order that Scripture might be fulfilled, Jesus said,
All:	"**I thirst.**"

Silent prayer or meditative comment or prepared prayer may follow.

Minister:	Have mercy on us, O Lord.
All:	**Jesus, we believe in you, we hope in you, we love you.** **Through your cross you brought us the hope of resurrection.**

Song: **Whatsoever You Do**, verses 1, 10.

VI

John 19:30

Narrator: There was a vessel filled with common wine. So they put a
sponge soaked in wine on a sprig of hyssop and put it up to
[Jesus'] mouth. When Jesus had taken the wine, he said,

All: **"It is finished."**

Silent prayer or meditative comment or prepared prayer may follow.

Minister: Have mercy on us, O Lord.

All: **Jesus, we believe in you, we hope in you, we love you.
Through your cross you brought us the hope of resurrection.**

Song: **O Sacred Head, Surrounded**, verses 1-2.

VII

Luke 23:44-46

Narrator: It was now about noon and darkness came over the whole land
until three in the afternoon because of an eclipse of the sun.
Then the veil of the temple was torn down the middle. Jesus
cried out in a loud voice,

All: **"Father, into your hands I commend my spirit."**

Silent prayer or meditative comment or prepared prayer may follow.

Minister: Have mercy on us, O Lord.

All: **Jesus, we believe in you, we hope in you, we love you.
Through your cross you brought us the hope of resurrection.**

Song: **Priestly People**, verses 1-2.

Homily

Concluding Rite

Litany

Minister: *All:*

Jesus, Son of the living God,   **Lord, save your people.**

Jesus, Son of the sorrowing Mother,	**Lord, save your people.**
Jesus, light of the world,	**Lord, save your people.**
Jesus, burning with love for us,	**Lord, save your people.**
Jesus, abandoned by your disciples,	**Lord, save your people.**
Jesus, suffering on the cross,	**Lord, save your people.**
Jesus, obedient unto death,	**Lord, save your people.**
Jesus, rising to new life,	**Lord, save your people.**
Jesus, salvation of us all,	**Lord, save your people.**
Jesus, our peace and reconciliation,	**Lord, save your people.**

Dismissal

Minister: I will not leave you orphans;
I will come to you.   Jn 14:18

All: **Holy God, mighty God, ever-living God, have mercy on us.**

Minister: Go in peace to serve the Lord in one another.

All: **Thanks be to God.**

Closing Song: **Yes, I Shall Arise** or any suitable song.

Lent's Meaning—
Penitential Service

Introductory Rites

Opening Song: **Draw Near, O Lord** or any suitable song.

Call to Worship

Minister: I take no pleasure in the death of the wicked man, says the
Lord,
but rather in the wicked man's conversion, that he may live.

Ez 33:11

All: **Merciful and gracious is the LORD**
slow to anger and abounding in kindness.   Ps 103:8

Minister: Return to the LORD, your God.
For gracious and merciful is he.   Jl 2:13

All: **Not according to our sins does he deal with us,**
nor does he requite us according to our crimes.

Ps 103:10

Opening Prayer

Minister: Let us pray.
Father, help us to live this season of Lent as a time of reflection,
confession and thanksgiving, and a new dedication to your Son
whose passion we remember. Be with us as we pray and sing,
think and resolve.

We ask this through Christ our Lord.

All: **Amen.**

Reading of the Word of God

First Reading: Joel 2:12-18 (L886-3)
[Return to the Lord with your whole heart.]

Response: Psalm 51:1-2, 3-4ab, 10-11, 12 and 15 (L888-1)
   R.   Be merciful, O Lord, for we have sinned.

Second Reading: 1 John 1:5 — 2:2 (L887-2)

[If we acknowledge our sins, God will forgive us.]

Gospel: Luke 9:22-25 (L221)

[What gain is it to win the whole world and lose our very selves?]

Homily

Intercessions

Minister: My brothers and sisters,
we should pray at all times,
but especially during this season of Lent:
we should faithfully keep watch with Christ and pray to our
Father.

Reader: That Christians everywhere may be responsive to the word of
God during this holy season, we pray to the Lord.

R. Lord, hear our prayer.

That people everywhere may work for peace to make these
days the acceptable time of God's help and salvation, we pray
to the Lord.   **R.**

That all who have sinned or grown lukewarm may turn to God
again during this time of reconciliation, we pray to the Lord.   **R.**

That we ourselves may learn to repent and turn from sin with
all our hearts, we pray to the Lord.   **R.**

We may pause to add our own intentions, concluding each with the response.

Minister: Lord, may your people turn again to you
and serve you with all their hearts.
With confidence we have asked your help;
may we now know your mercy and love in our lives.

We ask this through Christ our Lord.

All: **Amen.**

Other Lenten formulas appear in the Sacramentary, *Appendix 1, nos. 6 and 7.*

Resolution

All: **Father of infinite mercy and compassion,**
we recognize the truth
of your persistent love and acceptance.
We recognize our frailties and limits
in finding the inner harmony and personal integrity
for which our human hearts so ardently yearn.
By the power of your Spirit,
help us to turn to your Son, Jesus,
present in the community of faith,
for the reconciling power he alone can give.
Heal the wounds and hurts that divide us.
Renew our minds and hearts
as people bound to you in covenant.
Let us experience a genuine inner conversion
from the paralysis of sin
so that with all your saints
we may live in the freedom of your children,
acknowledging the dominion of Jesus' power in our lives.
May we find in the sacrament of reconciliation
an experience of worship in spirit and in truth,
so that we may ever proclaim our eucharistic praise
of your healing acceptance and transforming love.
Amen.

Concluding Rite

Minister: Father, bless our living of this Lenten season.
Let the great day at its end
flood all the days between with Easter hope,
so that our observance may not darken into gloom
but may remain bright with its promise.
We pray in the name of Jesus Christ,
your dying and rising Son.

All: **Amen.**

Blessing

Minister: The Father of mercies has given us an example of unselfish love
in the sufferings of his only Son.

Through our service of God and neighbor
may we receive countless blessings.

All: **Amen.**

Minister: We believe that by his dying
Christ destroyed death forever.
May he give us everlasting life.

All: **Amen.**

Minister: He humbled himself for our sakes.
May we follow his example
and share in his resurrection.

All: **Amen.**

A priest or deacon adds:

May almighty God bless you,
the Father, and the Son and the Holy Spirit.

All: **Amen.**

Closing Song: **These Forty Days of Lent** or any suitable song.

Now Is the Acceptable Time—
Penitential Service

Introductory Rites

Opening Song: **This Is Our Accepted Time** or **Grant to Us, O Lord** or any suitable song.

Call to Celebration

Minister: Delay not your conversion to the LORD,
             put it not off from day to day.   Sir 5:8

All: **Let us search and examine our ways**
             that we may return to the LORD!   Lam 3:40

Opening Prayer

Minister: Let us pray.

             Merciful Lord,
             we ask forgiveness of our sins.
             Help us as we hear your scriptures
             to heed your invitation to repent.
             May we see ourselves in need of your mercy.
             Help us to make Lent a preparation
             for the glory that is to come.

             We ask this through Christ our Lord.

All: **Amen.**

Reading of the Word of God

First Reading: Hosea 14:2-3; 10
    [Hosea invites us to repentance.]

Response:

Reader: Your word, O LORD, endures forever;
             it is firm as the heavens.   Ps 119:89

All: **My soul weeps for sorrow;**
             strengthen me according to your words.   Ps 119:28

Reader: A lamp to my feet is your word,
a light to my path.   Ps 119:105

Gospel: John 20:19-23 (L64)

   [Jesus brings peace and forgiveness.]

Response: **Draw Near, O Lord** or **Hosea** or any suitable song.

Homily

Litany

Minister: Behold, now is a very acceptable time;
Behold, now is the day of salvation.   2 Cor 6:2

All: **The kindness of God leads us to repentance.**   cf. Rom 2:4

Minister: Come now, let us set things right,
   says the LORD.
Though your sins be like scarlet,
   they may become white as snow.   Is 1:18

All: **Cleanse me of sin, . . .**
   that I may be purified;
wash me, and I shall be whiter than snow.   Ps 51:9

Minister: Come, let us walk in the light of the Lord!

All: **The night is advanced, the day is at hand.**
Let us then throw off the works of darkness
[and] put on the armor of light.   Rom 13:12

Resolution

Minister: Our God acts not by caprice but by careful design. Thus all the
important acts of salvation have followed a period of
purification and preparation.

All: **There is an appointed time for everything,**
   and a time for every affair under the heavens.   Eccl 3:1

Minister: Before the covenant with the human race was made to Noah, a period of rain separated the just from the unjust.

All: **For forty days and forty nights
heavy rain poured down on the earth.**   Gen 7:12

Minister: Before the covenant was given on Mount Sinai,
Moses underwent a period of preparation.

All: **Moses passed into the midst of the cloud
as he went up on the mountain;
and there he stayed for forty days and forty nights.**

Ex 24:18

Minister: Before the prophet Elijah could commune with God,
he had to undergo a period of pilgrimage.

All: **He got up, ate and drank;
then strenthened by that food,
he walked forty days and forty nights
to the mountain of God.**   1 Kgs 19:8

Minister: Before the beginning of his public ministry, Jesus experienced a period of testing in the desert.

All: **Filled with the Holy Spirit, Jesus returned from the Jordan and
was led by the Spirit into the desert for forty days, to be
tempted by the devil.**   Lk 4:1

Minister: Before his return to the Father, the risen Lord prepared the disciples for the church's mission.

All: **He presented himself alive to them by many proofs after he
had suffered, appearing to them during forty days and
speaking to them about the kingdom of God.**   Acts 1:3

Minister: Now we are gathered to celebrate another period of forty days, a period of preparation whose goal is the glory of Easter.

All: **Let us rid ourselves of every burden and sin that clings to us
and persevere in running the race that lies before us; while
keeping our eyes fixed on Jesus, the leader and perfecter of
faith.**   Heb 12:1-2

Concluding Rite

Minister: The one who began a good work in you will continue to
complete it, until the day of Christ Jesus. Phil 1:6

All: **Blessed be the God and Father of our Lord Jesus Christ, who
has blessed us in Christ with every spiritual blessing.** Eph 1:3

Closing Song: **These Forty Days of Lent** or any suitable song.

EASTER AND PENTECOST

Joy at Easter — Prayer Service

Introductory Rites

The Easter candle stands lighted in a prominent place.

Isaiah foretold,

> The people who walked in darkness
>   have seen a great light;
> Upon those who dwelt in the land of gloom
>   a light has shone.
> You have brought them abundant joy and great rejoicing,
> As they rejoice before you (9:1).

The Easter Proclamation sings of mystery accomplished beyond the hope of the prophets: In the joyful announcement of the resurrection, even human suffering finds itself transformed, while the fullness of joy springs from the victory of the crucified Jesus, from his pierced heart and his glorified body. This victory enlightens the darkness of souls.

Opening Song: **At the Lamb's High Feast** or **Crown Him With Many Crowns** or any suitable song.

Call to Worship   (adapted from the Exsultet)

Minister: My friends, standing in the brightness of this holy light, join with me in prayer to almighty God.

All: **We ask that he show us mercy.**

Minister: Rejoice, Mother Church, made radiant by so great a light!

All: **Let this place ring out with rejoicing,
with the song of all of us gathered here.**

Reading of the Word of God

First Reading: Pope Paul VI, *Christian Joy*, May 9, 1975
   [Joy in the Resurrection]

Reader: A reading from the *Apostolic Exhortation on Christian Joy*.

Jesus accepts death at the hands of the wicked, death on a cross, to eradicate from human hearts the sins of self-sufficiency and to manifest to the Father a complete filial obedience. But the Father does not allow death to keep him in its power. Jesus' resurrection is the seal the Father places on the value of his Son's sacrifice: it is the proof of the Father's fidelity, according to the desire Jesus expressed before he entered into his Passion: "Father, give glory to your Son that your Son may give glory to you" (Jn 17:1). Henceforth, Jesus is living for ever in the glory of the Father, and this is why the disciples were confirmed in an ineradicable joy when they saw the Lord on Easter evening at Emmaus.

Here ends the reading. **Thanks be to God.**

Response: **Ye Sons and Daughters** or any suitable song.

Gospel: John 20:19-31 (L44)

[Joy in Jesus' presence]

The greeting of peace may follow this reading.

Homily

Resolution

(adapted from the Exsultet)

Sing a familiar Alleluia as a response after each statement.

Minister: Let us acclaim the unseen God, our all powerful Father, and his only son, our risen Lord Jesus Christ.

Reader: Jesus shed his blood for us and paid the debt of Adam's sin to our eternal Father. **R.**

We have celebrated the paschal feast, the slaying of the Lamb whose blood hallows the houses of the faithful. **R.**

God brought our ancestors, the children of Israel, dry-shod through the Red Sea in the flight from Egypt. **R.**

The light of the pillar of fire destroyed the darkness of sin. **R.**

Christians everywhere are cleansed from sin, restored to grace and united in holiness. **R.**

The holiness of Easter banishes wickedness, restores innocence to the fallen, puts hatred to flight, brings peace and humbles pride. **R.**

Minister: Father, how wondrous your mercy toward us,
how far beyond understanding your loving affection!
Therefore, holy Father, in the joy of this Easter
season accept our praise and thanks.
Through Christ, our risen Lord.

All: **Amen.**

Concluding Rite

Blessing   (adapted from the Exsultet)

Minister: May Jesus, the Morning Star that never sets,
find his light still burning in our lives.

All: **Amen.**

Minister: May Jesus who came back from the grave
shed his serene light upon all people.

All: **Amen.**

Minister: May the Father, the Son, and the Spirit fill us with joy, and may
we praise God with joyful hearts.

All: **Amen.**

Closing Song: **Jesus Christ Is Risen Today** or any suitable song.

Hope—Penitential Service

Introductory Rites

Opening Song: **Lord of All Hopefulness** or any suitable song.

Call to Worship

Minister: With God is my safety and my glory.

All: **He is the rock of my strength; my refuge is in God.**

Ps 62:8

Minister: Trust in him at all times, O my people!
Pour out your hearts before him.

All: **God is our refuge!**

Ps 62:9

Opening Prayer

Minister: Let us pray.

Merciful God,
your Son's cross has freed us.
In our frailty we have misused the gift of freedom.
We seek deliverance from the slavery of sin.
Help us to grow in the love of your commandments,
that in obedience to your will we may find perfect freedom.

We ask this through Christ our Lord.

All: **Amen**.

Reading of the Word of God

First Reading: *The Church in the Modern World*, No. 21
[Hope sustains us.]

Reader: A reading from the Second Vatican Council's *Pastoral Constitution on the Church in the Modern World*.

The Church holds that the recognition of God is in no way hostile to human dignity, since this dignity is rooted and perfected in God. For we were made as intelligent and free members of society by the God who created us. Even more importantly, we are called as children to commune with God and to share in his happiness. She further teaches that a hope related to the end of time does not diminish the importance of intervening duties, but rather undergirds the acquittal of them with fresh incentives. By contrast, when a divine substructure and the hope of eternal life are wanting, human dignity is most grievously lacerated, as current events often attest. The riddle of life and death, of guilt and of grief go unsolved, with the frequent result that people succumb to despair.

Here ends the reading.   **Thanks be to God.**

Response: **O God, Our Help in Ages Past** or any suitable song.

Gospel: John 14:1-3, 18-19
[We hope in Jesus' promises.]

Response: **Alleluia! Sing to Jesus!** or any suitable song.

Homily

Resolution

Minister: Let us rejoice in hope;
let us be patient under trial;
let us persevere in prayer.   cf. Rom 12:12

Reader: As we strive to admonish the sinner,
and as we are aware of our sins:

R.   We trust in your help, O Lord.

As we attempt to instruct the ignorant,
and as we admit our own ignorance of God and his ways:
R.

As we try to counsel the doubtful,
and as we attempt to live with our doubts:
R.

As we seek to comfort the sorrowful,
and as we succumb to self-pity:
R.

As we strive to bear wrongs patiently,
and as we find it hard to forgive all injuries:
R.

As we are mindful of the living and the dead,
and as we pray for their eternal happiness:
R.

Minister: God our Creator,
you cleanse us in the regeneration of baptism and purify us in
the sacrament of reconciliation.
Strengthen our profession of trust in your Son
whose promises deserve our trust.
Help us to rouse one another to generosity and service,
that we may encourage all
by our example of faith, hope and love.

We ask this through Christ our Lord.

All: **Amen**.

Concluding Rite

Dismissal

Minister: Christ was faithful as a son placed over [God's] house.
We are his house

All: **if [only] we hold fast to our confidence and pride in our
hope.**   Heb 3:6

Closing Song: **Give Thanks and Remember** or any suitable song.

Home Service for Pentecost

Scripture and the liturgy provide many ideas for a family celebration of this feast day. The color red is in great prominence. Fire and the dove are two well-recognized symbols of the Holy Spirit. Scriptural references to wind suggest a mobile with a dove and paper tongues of fire to decorate the dining room. The number of flames might correspond to the number of people who will share the meal. On each flame there might be written the name of each person, with the dates of baptism and confirmation, if known. If a mobile is not made, then the paper tongues of fire might be used as place cards. A special Pentecost cake might be made with twelve red candles representing the apostles, or seven candles for the seven gifts of the Holy Spirit. The number of candles might correspond to the number present at the meal. Red flowers and red candles in a seven-branched candelabrum might decorate the table or buffet.

Opening Prayer

Leader: Come, Holy Spirit, fill the hearts of your faithful.

All: **And kindle in them the fire of your love.**

Leader: LORD, send out your Spirit.

All: **And renew the face of the earth.** Ps 104:30

Leader: Let us pray.
Holy God,
bless our family, [our guests,]
our food and our celebration.
May all that we do today celebrate the coming of your Spirit.
Help us to live in the strength and grace of the Spirit who came to us in baptism and confirmation.

We ask this through Christ our Lord.

All: **Amen.**

Meal

At the conclusion of the meal, while the family sings a Pentecost song such as **Come, Holy Ghost** or **Sing Praise to Our Creator**, the cake can be brought in. Depending on the number of candles on the cake, as each is extinguished there may be a prayer for each person present, or for each gift of the Holy Spirit, or for the assistance of each of the apostles.

Closing Prayer

Leader: After the Holy Spirit descended on the apostles, they spoke of the wonderful works of the Lord. As a reminder of God's wonderful works in us, let us treasure the dates of our baptism and confirmation while we celebrate the coming of the Holy Spirit to the church and to ourselves.

Let us pray.

Father,
we thank you for this meal, this feast, this celebration.
Protect us who have been marked
with the sign of the cross in baptism and confirmation.
Let us treasure your gifts,
especially the Holy Spirit,
the first gift of the risen Lord.
By keeping your commandments,
may we all attain the glory of heaven
to which you have called us
through baptism and the Holy Spirit.

We ask this through Christ our Lord.

All: **Amen.**

The leader makes the sign of the cross on himself or herself and says:

May God bless us all,
the Father, and the Son, and the Holy Spirit.

All: **Amen.**

Pentecost—
Season for Renewal

Introductory Rites

The idea of renewal or change might appear contradictory to the nature of Christianity. But Jesus warned us about a too exclusive attachment to the past: ''No one who sets a hand to the plow and looks to what was left behind is fit for the kingdom of God'' (Lk 9:62). Pope John XXIII hoped that the Second Vatican Council would be a second Pentecost for the church. The season of Pentecost seems a fitting time to be true to his vision, that is, to renew our own intentions of renewal. In an age when we are more and more aware of progress, stability can be stagnancy. Cardinal Newman wrote, ''To live is to change, and to be perfect is to have changed often.'' So we seek the Spirit to ''renew the face of the earth'' (Ps 104:30).

Opening Song: **Come Holy Ghost** or **Grant to Us, O Lord** or any suitable song.

Proclamation of Renewal   (Eccl 3:1-8; Pope Paul VI)

Minister: There is an appointed time for everything,

All: **and a time for every affair under the heavens.**

Minister: A time to be born,

All: **and a time to die.**

Minister: A time to plant,

All: **and a time to uproot the plant.**

Minister: A time to kill,

All: **and a time to heal.**

Minister: A time to tear down,

All: **and a time to build.**

Minister: A time to weep,

All: **and a time to laugh.**

Minister: A time to mourn,

All: **and a time to dance.**

Minister: A time to scatter stones,

All: **and a time to gather them.**

Minister: A time to embrace,

All: **and a time to be far from embraces.**

Minister: A time to seek,

All: **and a time to lose.**

Minister: A time to keep,

All: **and a time to cast away.**

Minister: A time to rend,

All: **and a time to sew.**

Minister: A time to be silent,

All: **and a time to speak.**

Minister: A time to love,

All: **and a time to hate.**

Minister: A time of war,

All: **and a time of peace.**

Minister: A time to reawaken, reform, rejuvenate the church,

All: **to enlighten her conscience, to strengthen her forces, to purify her defects.**

Minister: A time to strengthen her structures,

All: **to widen her frontiers, to recompose her unity.**

Minister: A time to prepare her for new defense and new contacts with the world,

All: **to place her in renewed contact with her own sources.**

Minister: A time to hasten her fruitful journey toward her final goal,

All: **the glorious meeting with Jesus her Lord.**

Reading of the Word of God

First Reading: Genesis 11:1-9 (L63)

[Babel was a human attempt at renewal.]

Response: Sirach 10:12-13, 16-17

> **The beginning of pride is man's stubbornness**
> **in withdrawing his heart from his Maker;**
> **For pride is the reservoir of sin,**
> **a source which runs over with vice;**
> **Because of it God sends unheard-of afflictions**
> **and brings men to utter ruin.**
> **He breaks down their stem to the level of the ground,**
> **then digs their roots from the earth.**
> **The traces of the proud God sweeps away**
> **and effaces the memory of them from the earth.**

Second Reading: Acts 2:1-11 (L64)

[The Spirit brought renewal to human hearts.]

Response: **All You Nations** or **The Spirit of God** or any suitable song.

Homily

Resolution

Minister: Come, Spirit of the new creation,
make us into a renewed people.

All: **Spirit of God, gift of God, fill us with your life.**

Minister: Come, spouse of the church,
and help us to be instruments in its renewal.

All: **Spirit of God, gift of God, fill us with your life.**

Minister: Spirit of the promise,
remain with us in peace all our days.

All: **Spirit of God, gift of God, fill us with your life.**

Concluding Rite

Dismissal

Minister: Those who are led by the Spirit of God are children of God.

Rom 8:14

All: **This Spirit he richly poured out on us**
through Jesus Christ our Savior,
so that we might be justified by his grace
and become heirs in hope of eternal life.   Ti 3:6-7

A priest or deacon adds:

Go forth in the name of God: Father, Son and Holy Spirit.

All: **Amen.**

Closing Song: **Go Forth** or **God's Blessing Sends Us Forth** or any suitable song.

IN THE SPIRIT—
SCRIPTURE SERVICE

Introductory Rites

Commentator: The sacrament of baptism gave us our birth in the faith. The sacrament of confirmation has strengthened us in faith. Both have pledged us to lead a dedicated life, giving testimony to Jesus by our actions. Let us renew the Christian pledge represented in these two sacraments and call upon the Holy Spirit to renew his grace in us.

Opening Song: **Come, Holy Ghost** or any suitable song.

Greeting

Minister: Let us trace the sign of the cross on our + foreheads, on our + lips, and over our + hearts. We put our trust in heavenly teaching and pray to lead a life that may truly fit us to be a dwelling place for God.

Opening Prayer

Minister: Let us pray.

Almighty, everlasting God,
look with favor on us
who took our first steps in the faith through baptism.
Rid us of all inward blindness,
and sever the snares of Satan which may have entangled us.
Open wide for us the door of your embracing love.
May the seal of your wisdom so penetrate us
as to cast out all evil inclinations
and let in the fragrance of your holy teachings.
Thus shall we serve you in your church
and daily grow in your grace.

We ask this through Christ our Lord.

All: **Amen.**

or

The minister may invite the congregation to extend their hands during the prayer for the gifts of the Holy Spirit.

Minister: Almighty and eternal God, Father of our Lord Jesus Christ,
you caused us to be born again of water and the Holy Spirit,
and you pardoned all our sins.
Pour out upon us your Holy Spirit, the Paraclete,
with his seven gifts.

All: **Amen.**

Minister: The Spirit of wisdom and understanding!

All: **Amen.**

Minister: The Spirit of right judgment and courage!

All: **Amen.**

Minister: The Spirit of knowledge and reverence!

All: **Amen.**

Minister: The Spirit of wonder and awe in your presence!

All: **Amen.**

Reading of the Word of God

First Reading: Acts 2:1-11 (L64)

[Filled with the Holy Spirit, the apostles proclaimed God's marvelous deeds.]

Response:

All: **Strengthen, O God, what you have begun in us.**
You gave your apostles the Holy Spirit,
ordaining that they and their successors
should hand down that gift to the faithful.
Look with favor on us
whose foreheads have been anointed with chrism
and sealed with the sign of the cross.
May the Holy Spirit consecrate our hearts
as a fitting dwelling for your glory.

Gospel: John 14:23-26 (L767-10)

[The Father will give the Spirit to all who love and obey Jesus.]

Homily

Thanks and Commitment

Minister: The Holy Spirit has been given to us to recall and to complete the teachings of Jesus in the church and in our personal lives, in order to maintain our faith and our pledge of apostolic witness.

Reader: Reborn as children of God in baptism, we confess the faith we have received through the church. For this we give thanks.

R. We thank you, Lord.

By the sacrament of confirmation we are more perfectly committed to the church. For this we give thanks. **R.**

The Holy Spirit endows us with special strength to spread the faith in word and action as true witnesses of Jesus. For this we give thanks. **R.**

As the people of God we share also in Jesus' prophetic office. For this we give thanks. **R.**

The Holy Spirit leads and sanctifies the people of God, allotting his gifts to everyone as he wills. For this we give thanks. **R.**

By his gifts the Holy Spirit makes us ready for the work of building up the church. For this we give thanks. **R.**

Commentator: In baptism and confirmation the sign of the cross was traced on our foreheads. The minister will trace the cross on us once again as a sign that we put our whole trust in Jesus, and as a pledge that we will lead lives which may truly fit us to be a dwelling place for God.

All may approach the minister and then return to their places.

Minister: Receive the sign of the cross on your + forehead and in your heart.

All: **Amen.**

Concluding Rite

Minister: Let us pray.

Lord God,
hear our prayer and protect your chosen ones.
We have been marked with the sign of the Savior's holy cross.
Let us treasure this sharing

by living your teaching and keeping your commandments.
May we attain the glory of heaven
to which we are called by new birth in water
and the Holy Spirit.

We ask this through Christ our Lord.

All: **Amen.**

Minister: Go in peace to love and serve the Lord.

All: **Thanks be to God.**

Closing Song: **The Spirit of God** or any suitable song.

SPIRIT OF JOY — PRAYER SERVICE

Introductory Rites

Opening Song: **Come, Holy Ghost** or any suitable song.

Call to Worship

Minister: LORD, send out your Spirit.

All: **And renew the face of the earth.**   Ps 104:30

Minister: Come, Holy Spirit, fill the hearts of your faithful.

All: **And kindle in them the fire of your love.**

Reading of the Word of God

First Reading: Pope Paul VI, *Christian Joy*, May 9, 1975.
    [The Spirit is the source of hope.]

Reader: A reading from the *Apostolic Exhortation on Christian Joy*.

Paschal joy is the joy of the new presence of the risen Christ
dispensing to his own the Holy Spirit, so that he may dwell with
them. The Holy Spirit is given to the Church to be the inexhaustible
principle of her joy as the bride of the glorified Christ. The Christian
knows that this spirit will never be quenched in the course of history.
The source of hope manifested at Pentecost will never be exhausted.

Here ends the reading.   **Thanks be to God.**

All pause for a few moments of silent reflection.

Gospel: John 20:19-23 (L64)
    [The Spirit empowers the ministry of reconciliation.]

Response: **Joyful, Joyful, We Adore Thee** or any suitable song.

Second Reading: Pope Paul VI, *Christian Joy*, May 9, 1975.
    [The spirit is the source of all joy.]

Reader: A reading from the *Apostolic Exhortation on Christian Joy.*

The Holy Spirit raises up in our hearts a filial prayer that is expressed in praise, thanksgiving, reparation and supplication. Then we can experience joy which is properly spiritual, the joy which is a fruit of the Holy Spirit. The humble human joys of our lives are transfigured. Here below this joy will always include the painful trial of a woman in travail, and a certain apparent abandonment like that of the orphan: tears and lamentation, while the world parades its gloating satisfaction. But the disciples' sadness, which is according to God and not according to the world, will be promptly changed into a spiritual joy that no one will be able to take away from them.

Here ends the reading.   **Thanks be to God.**

All pause for a few moments of silent reflection.

Gospel: John 16:12-15, 20-23 (L293 & 295)
[The Spirit guides us all to truth.]

Response: **I Will Bless the Lord at All Times** or **Amazing Grace** or any suitable song.

Homily

Resolution

(Pentecost Sequence)

Sing a familiar Alleluia or Holy Spirit refrain as a response after each statement.

Minister: Come, Holy Spirit,
and from heaven direct on us
the rays of your light.   **R.**

Come, Father of the poor;
come, giver of God's gifts;
come, light of our hearts.   **R.**

Kindly Paraclete,
in your gracious visits to the soul
you bring relief and consolation.   **R.**

If it is weary with toil, you bring it ease;
in the heat of temptation, your grace cools it;
if sorrowful, your words console it.   **R.**

Light most blessed,
shine on the hearts of your faithful—
even into their darkest corners;   **R.**

For without your aid
we can do nothing good,
and everything is sinful.   **R.**

Wash clean the sinful soul,
rain down your grace on the parched soul
and heal the injured soul.   **R.**

Soften the hard heart,
cherish and warm the ice-cold heart,
and give direction to the wayward.   **R.**

Give your seven holy gifts to your faithful,
for their trust is in you.   **R.**

Give them reward for their virtuous acts;
give them a death that ensures salvation;
give them unending bliss.   **R.**

Concluding Rite

Blessing

Minister: May the God of hope,
fill you with all joy and peace in believing,
so that you may abound in hope
by the power of the Holy Spirit.   Rom 15:13

All: **Amen.**

A priest or deacon adds:

May almighty God bless us,
the Father, and the Son, and the Holy Spirit.

All: **Amen.**

Closing Song: **Jerusalem, My Happy Home** or **God's Blessing Sends Us Forth** or
any suitable song.

Jesus in Glory— Penitential Service

Introductory Rites

Commentator: Jesus said, "When I am lifted up from earth, I will draw everyone to myself" (Jn 12:32). This service provides an occasion for us to renew our intention to live according to this divine attraction, which seeks from us a total response in faith and action. Realizing our weaknesses and failings of the past weeks, we come together to ask Jesus' forgiveness and assistance in renewing our baptismal commitment to faith and Christian living.

Opening Song: **Alleluia! Sing to Jesus!** or any suitable song.

Call to Worship

Minister: Since we have a great high priest
who has passed through the heavens,
Jesus, the Son of God,
let us hold fast to our confession.   Heb 4:14

All: [He] was manifested in the flesh,
vindicated in the Spirit,
seen by the angels,
proclaimed to the Gentiles,
believed in throughout the world,
taken up in glory.   1 Tim 3:16

Opening Prayer

Minister: Let us pray.

Loving God,
you sent Jesus to save us.
Help us now to express our sorrow,
ask forgiveness and renew

our faith in Jesus' victory over sin,
so that one day we too may be with you forever.

We ask this through Christ our Lord.

All:　　　　**Amen.**

Reading of the Word of God

First Reading:　Hebrews 7:25 — 8:1 (L314, partial)
　　[Jesus is our Mediator.]

Response:　Hebrews 9:27, 24, 28

All:　　　　**Just as it is appointed that [we] die once,**
　　　　　and after this the judgment,
　　　　　so also Christ, offered once
　　　　　to take away the sins of many.
　　　　　[He entered] heaven itself
　　　　　that he might now appear before God on our behalf.
　　　　　[He] will appear a second time, not to take away sin
　　　　　but to bring salvation to those who eagerly await him.

Second reading:　Colossians 3:1-11 (L439-1)
　　[Prepare for Jesus' return.]

Response:　**Keep in Mind** or any suitable song.

Homily

Resolution

(*Te Deum*)

Minister:　Before returning to faith in action, we join our praise to that of
　　　　all creation.

All:　　　　**You are God: we praise you;**
　　　　　You are the Lord: we acclaim you;
　　　　　You are the eternal Father:
　　　　　All creation worships you.

　　　　　To you all angels, all the powers of heaven,
　　　　　Cherubim and Seraphim, sing in endless praise:
　　　　　　　Holy, holy, holy Lord, God of power and might,
　　　　　　　heaven and earth are full of your glory.

The glorious company of apostles praise you.
The noble fellowship of prophets praise you.
The white-robed army of martyrs praise you.

Throughout the world the holy Church acclaims you:
    Father, of majesty unbounded,
    your true and only Son, worthy of all worship,
    and the Holy Spirit, advocate and guide.

You, Christ, are the king of glory,
the eternal Son of the Father.
When you became man to set us free
you did not shun the Virgin's womb.

You overcame the sting of death,
and opened the kingdom of heaven to all believers.
You are seated at God's right hand in glory.
We believe that you will come and be our judge.

Come then, Lord, and help your people,
bought with the price of your own blood,
and bring us with your saints
to glory everlasting.

Minister: Save your people, [LORD,] and bless your inheritance.

Ps 28:9

All: **Govern and uphold them now and always.**

Minister: Day by day we bless you.

All: **We praise your name for ever.**

Minister: Keep us today, Lord, from all sin.

All: **Have mercy on us, Lord, have mercy.**

Minister: Lord, show us your love and mercy;

All: **For we put our trust in you.**

Minister: In you, Lord, is our hope:

All: **And we shall never hope in vain.**

Concluding Rite

Dismissal   (Jude 1:24-25)

Minister: To the one who is able to keep you from stumbling
and to present you unblemished and exultant,
in the presence of his glory,
to the only God, our savior,
through Jesus Christ our Lord
be glory, majesty, power, and authority
from ages past, now, and for ages to come.

All: **Amen.**

Closing Song: **People of God, Rejoice!** or any suitable song.

PARISH
CELEBRATIONS

SERVICE FOR THE OPENING OF SCHOOL

The service may be adapted according to the grade levels of the students present. The service may be led by a priest, deacon or lay person.

This is a celebration to increase awareness, responsiveness, identity, friendship and unity as the new school year begins. It is helpful if the classes discuss these ideas and plan the program in their rooms. The program may occur in the school hall, the church or, if necessary, on the playground. Those to be introduced and those with speaking roles should assemble beforehand but teachers should remain with their classes. A public address system and seating for all are essential.

Introduction

Opening Comment

The principal or another staff member calls the assembly to order.

Opening Song

A well-known song invites full participation.

Welcome

The principal or pastor welcomes all back to school.

The principal presents the faculty and staff individually, emphasizing those who are new this year. They rise at their places, and applause ends the introductions.

If there is a school song, all may sing it. Likewise, if there is a school flag, it may be brought forward and its symbolism explained by an articulate older student. Banners and art prepared by the students may decorate the area. Introductions proceed as one or two other older students introduce all the new children in the school, assembled on the stage. The teachers will have to prepare name lists for these announcers. First grade or kindergarten children, remaining at their seats, are introduced as a class, since this is their first year in school.

The last segment of introductions calls forward the heads of various school organizations such as eighth grade officers, the leaders of the student council, patrol students, servers, scouts and other activities. If capable, these leaders could give appropriate comments on the role, privilege and responsibility of each organization. Applause occurs only once, at the conclusion of this segment.

A song of community, such as **Prayer of Saint Francis** *or* **Let There Be Peace on Earth** *emphasizes the part each must play to build school spirit. It will also prepare the assembly for the gospel reading.*

Reading of the Word of God

Gospel: John 17:1, 8, 11, 24, 26 passim

[Together in Christ]

Minister: [Jesus] raised his eyes to heaven and said, "Father, . . . the words you gave to me, I have given to them and they accepted them and truly understood that I came from you, and they have believed that you sent me . . . Holy Father, keep them in your name that you have given me, so that they may be one just as we are. . . . Father, they are your gift to me. I wish that where I am they also may be with me . . . that the love with which you loved me may be in them and I in them.

This is the gospel of the Lord.

All: **Praise to you, Lord Jesus Christ.**

Action

Minister: Not only must we be one with Jesus, but also with one another. The Bible says, "How good it is, and how pleasant, where friends dwell as one!" (Ps 133:1). As an expression of our unity, let us turn to those on either side and exchange greetings of welcome.

All greet those close to them in words and gestures of their own choice.

Intercessions

Each class will have formulated an intention. One student from each room comes forward to read it at the microphone. These intentions may petition for the staff, the students, support of programs, safety, health, joy, honesty, service, openness, hard work, etc. The response might be, "Lord, we ask you, hear our prayer," recited or set to music.

Minister: Let us now pray the words Jesus taught us.

All: **Our Father, . . .**

Conclusion

If the pastor or another priest is present, he may give a final blessing to the assembly:

> Grow in grace, and in the knowledge
> of our Lord and Savior Jesus Christ.

All: **Amen.**

> To him be glory forever and ever.

All: **Amen.**

> May almighty God bless you,
> the Father, and the Son, and the Holy Spirit.

All: **Amen.**

Closing Song

A song of community, such as **Whatsoever You Do** *or* **Seek Ye First** continues the thematic unity of the program as the younger classes begin to exit.

Celebration

On return to the classrooms, treats might be passed out. Written contests might be held, and prizes awarded to the student in each room who can name the most faculty and staff members, or all the new students in the homeroom, etc.

Service to Close the School Year

The service may be adapted according to the grade levels of the students present. The service may be led by a priest, deacon or lay person.

Introductory Rites

Opening Song: **All That I Am** or any suitable song.

All with leading roles go in procession to the sanctuary or stage.

Call to Celebration

Minister:	It is good to give thanks to the Lord
	to sing praise to [his] name.

Ps 92:1

All: **How great are your works, O Lord!**

Ps 92:6

Opening Prayer

Minister: Let us pray.

God in heaven,
we have discovered the beauty of your creation.
Fill us with thanks and loving respect
for life, nature and education.
May we use what we have learned this year
to praise you with Jesus and the Holy Spirit forever.

All: **Amen.**

Reading of the Word of God

First Reading: St. Francis of Assisi
[The Wonders of Creation]

Reader 1:   A reading from Saint Francis of Assisi.
O most high, omnipotent, good Lord God,
praise and glory, all honor and blessing are yours!

**R.   Praise and bless the Lord, all his creatures!
Give thanks to him and serve him with great humility.**

Reader 2: We praise you, Lord, for our brother the sun
who brings us the day and its light.
He is fair and radiant, shining in great splendor.   **R.**

Reader 3: We praise you, Lord, for our sister the moon,
and for the stars which you spread bright and lovely in the
heavens.   **R.**

Reader 4: We praise you, Lord, for our brother the wind,
and for air and cloud, calms and all weather,
by which you uphold life in all creation.   **R.**

Reader 5: We praise you, Lord, for our sister the water
who is most serviceable to us, humble, precious and chaste.   **R.**

Reader 6: We praise you, Lord, for our brother the fire
by whom you light up the night.
He is bright and cheerful, mighty and strong.   **R.**

Reader 7: We praise you, Lord, for our mother the earth
who sustains us and keeps us
and brings forth many fruits, colorful flowers and foliage.   **R.**

Reader 8: We praise you, Lord, for those
who pardon one another for your sake
and who bear weakness and tribulation.   **R.**

Reader 9: Blest are they who shall walk by your most holy will,
for you, the Most High, shall give them a crown.   **R.**

Response: **Praise God in His Creation** or any suitable song.

Gospel: Matthew 5:14-16
[Praise in Action]

Homily

Sign of Commitment

Minister: During this school year we tried to strengthen our faith, hope
and love by Christian study and action. To show our intention
of continuing our growth throughout the summer, let us give
one another a greeting of peace.

All greet those close to them in words and gestures of their own choice.

Song of Peace: **He Is Lord** or any suitable song.

Intercessions

Minister: Before we leave for our summer vacations, we will pray with
one another and for one another.

*Each class will have formulated an intention. To avoid repetition, prior consultation among
the teachers is helpful. One student from each room comes forward to read the intention
into the microphone. The intentions may petition for the staff, students, summer safety,
health, joy, honesty, service, openness, enjoyable vacations, etc.*

Minister: Loving God, go with us on our way
as we try to live each day for you and for others.

We pray through Christ our Lord.

All: **Amen.**

Conclusion

Dismissal

Minister: Go in peace and let your light shine before the world,
so that all may see your goodness
and give praise to your heavenly Father.   Mt 5:16

All: **Thanks be to God.**

Closing Song: **You Fill the Day** or **Thank You, Lord** or any suitable song.

Prayers for a Parish Meeting

Opening

Minister: Let us pray for God's help
and the inspiration of the Holy Spirit during our meeting.

Reading: 2 Corinthians 4:13-15

[We come together in faith and love to serve the Lord in our community.]

Response:

All: **I will state directly what is in my mind,**
my lips shall utter knowledge sincerely;
For the spirit of God has made me,
the breath of the Almighty keeps me alive.   Job 33:3-4

Intercessions

Minister: We are gathered in the Spirit.
Let us open our minds and hearts to the needs of our parish.

Reader: That we may put aside any self-interest
in favor of the good of the whole parish community,
we pray to the Lord.   **Lord, hear our prayer.**

That each member of this
council/committee/society/association/body
may openly express ideas, problems and projects
for mature consideration by everyone present,
we pray to the Lord.   **Lord, hear our prayer.**

That our parish community may always respond
to the needs of all its members,
regardless of age or social status,
we pray to the Lord.   **Lord, hear our prayer.**

We may pause to add our own intentions, aloud or in silence.

Minister: Father, you have heard our prayer for your assistance.
We believe we are gathered here in your Spirit.
Strengthen our faith, hope and love,
and bring our efforts to a fruitful resolution.

We ask this through Christ our Lord.

All: **Amen.**

Closing

Reading: Ephesians 3:14-19 (L913-4)

[May we grasp the unbounded love of Christ.]

Response: Ephesians 3:20-21

All: **To him who is able to accomplish
far more than we ask or imagine,
by the power at work within us,
to him be glory in the church and in Christ Jesus
to all generations, forever and ever. Amen.**

If there is a priest present, he may impart a closing blessing.

SERVICE FOR TRAVEL

The blessing contained in the following service is not from an official church ritual. All gather together around the table or in the family room, after the vehicle is packed, just before departure.

Call to Worship

Leader: May [we] be blessed in the city,
             and blessed in the country!   Dt 28:3

All: **May [we] be blessed in our coming in,
         and blessed in our going out!**   Dt 28:6

Leader: Let us pray.

Lord, hear our prayers
and graciously accompany us in our travel.
Grant us a happy journey and a peaceful time,
that we may safely reach our destination,
return in joy to our home,
and come finally to the haven of eternal salvation.

We ask this through Christ our Lord.

All: **Amen.**

Opening Song: **America the Beautiful** or any suitable song.

Reading of the Word of God

Reading: Tobit 5:10, 16-17 passim

[Tobiah will travel safely in the angel Raphael's company.]

Reader: A reading from the book of Tobit.

Tobit said to Raphael: "My son Tobiah wants to go to Media. Can you go with him to show him the way?" Raphael answered: "Yes, I can go with him, for I know all the routes. I have often traveled to Media and crossed all its plains and mountains; so I know the road well. Have no fear. In good health we shall leave you, and in good health we shall return to you, for the way is safe." Then Tobit called his son and said to him: "Prepare whatever you need for the journey. May God in heaven protect you on the way and bring you back to me safe and sound; and may his angel accompany you for safety, my son."

Tobiah kissed his father and mother. Tobit said to him, "Have a safe journey."

This is the word of the Lord.   **Thanks be to God.**

Response: Psalm 121:5, 8

All: **The LORD is [our] guardian;. . .**
            he is beside [us] at [our] right hand.
            The LORD will guard [our] coming and [our] going,
            both now and forever.

Prayer

Leader: God has given his angels charge over us.

All: **To guard us in all our undertakings.**

Leader: Let us pray.

            O God, we marvel at your providence
            which has given your holy angels care over us.
            You sent the archangel Raphael
            to accompany Tobiah on his journey.
            Grant that he may also watch over us in our travels.
            May he present our prayers for your blessing,
            that we may be safe under his protection
            and happy in your company for all eternity.

            We ask this through Christ our Lord.

All: **Amen.**

Concluding Rite

Leader: May the almighty and merciful Lord
            lead us along ways of peace and contentment,
            and may the angel Raphael accompany us on our journey.

All: **So we may return to our home**
            in peace, health and joy.

Closing Song: **Now Thank We All Our God** or any suitable song.

Picnic Service

All gather around the table or the grill before mealtime.

Call to Celebration

Leader: God looked at everything he had made.

All: **And he found it very good.** Gen 1:31

Leader: Let us pray.

Lord our God, we celebrate this opportunity to be together, cheered by the love of one another and surrounded by the natural beauty of the earth. Let the things of earth refresh us and increase our awareness of the beauty in one another and in you.

We ask this through Christ our Lord.

All: **Amen.**

Opening Song: **You Fill the Day** or **Praise God in His Creation** or any suitable song.

Reading of the Word of God

Gospel: Matthew 6:26-33

[Believe in your heavenly Father and he will take care of your needs.]

Response: Sirach 39:14-16, 33, 35 passim

All: **Bless the LORD for all he has done!**
Proclaim the greatness of his name,
loudly sing his praises.
Sing out with joy as you proclaim:
The works of God are all of them good.

The works of God are all of them good;
every need when it comes he fills.
So now with full joy of heart proclaim
and bless the name of the Holy One.

Blessing of Fire and Food

Leader: [Our] help is from the LORD.

All:	**Who made heaven and earth.**	Ps 121:2

Leader: Let us pray.

O God, by your word all things are made holy.
Bless this fire and this food
[hamburgers, hotdogs, marshmallows, salad, cookies,
watermelon . . .]
which you have created.
Grant that whoever gives thanks to you
and uses them in accordance with your law and your will
may receive health of body and protection of soul
by calling on your holy name.

We ask this through Christ our Lord.

All: **Amen.**

Concluding Rite

At the close of the picnic, all help clean up the area to preserve the beauty of the earth for those who will come another day.

Litany

Choose from the following intentions those phrases that best describe the day's experiences. All present may add other expressions.

Leader: For this time to enjoy the earth,
one another and you, O Lord:

> **R. We thank you, Lord**, or any suitable response.

For the beautiful sight of sunshine and flowers,
grass and trees, butterflies and gliding birds: **R.**

For the delightful sounds of calling birds,
rushing water and crackling campfires: **R.**

For the enjoyable scents of fresh air,
roasting hotdogs and steaming coffee: **R.**

For the pleasant touch of grass and sand,
the warmth of the sun,
the stimulation of the wind and water: **R.**

For this time to re-create ourselves
in body, mind and spirit: **R.**

For the refreshment of exercise,
the calm away from the pressures of work: **R.**

For this relaxed time to renew the bonds of love
sometimes overlooked in the routine of daily work: **R.**

For all who try to make this earth a better place to live: **R.**

Departure

Leader: Let us return home refreshed in body and spirit.

All: **Thanks be to God.**

Closing Song: **Now Thank We All Our God** or **Stewards of Earth** or any suitable
song.

Home Service for Shut-Ins

Since 1972 the third Sunday of October has been designated as National Shut-In Day to express concern for the sick, the elderly, the handicapped and the imprisoned. This is a day for visiting and outings, knowing that the medicines of love and hope are most effective. If a priest makes the visitation, a home Mass may be a possibility.

Introductory Rites

Opening Song: **Where Charity and Love Prevail** or any suitable song.

Call to Celebration   (2 Cor 1:3-4)

Minister: Blessed be the Father of compassion and God of all encouragement.

All: **[He] encourages us in our every affliction, so that we may be able to encourage those who are in any affliction with the encouragement with which we ourselves are encouraged by God.**

The minister may invite all to greet one another with a sign of peace.

Opening Prayer

Minister: Let us pray.

Lord, we meet to enrich our understanding
of the call to be your servants.
Strengthen our faith, hope and love
through this sharing of thoughts and prayers.

We ask this through Christ our Lord.

All: **Amen.**

Reading of the Word of God

First Reading: Romans 8:18-30 (L877-1)
[Present sufferings are as nothing compared to future glory.]

Alternate readings:

Lamentations 3:17-26 (L876-2)
1 Corinthians 1:26-31 (L740-2)
2 Corinthians 4:10-18 (L872-2)
Hebrews 13:1-3, 14-16 (L867-3)
James 1:2-4, 12 (L877-3)

Response: **Whatsoever You Do** or **We Are the Light of the World** or any
suitable song.

Gospel: Matthew 11:28-30 (L184)
[Jesus refreshes the weary and burdened.]

Discussion

*We may share our thoughts on the readings. Instrumental music or a recording may
accompany silent reflection.*

Intercessions

Minister: Realizing our responsibility
to pray and show concern for one another,
we direct our petitions to Jesus:

Reader: For the ministers of the church,
that they may always serve the lonely and the isolated,
we pray to the Lord.   **Lord, hear our prayer.**

That local, state and national officials may always cooperate to
improve the quality of life for all people,
we pray to the Lord.   **Lord, hear our prayer.**

For the sick and dying,
the imprisoned and those suffering any need,
that we may show them our Christian concern,
we pray to the Lord.   **Lord, hear our prayer.**

We may pause to add our own intentions, aloud or in silence.

Minister: Let us renew our commitment to one another with the words
our Savior gave us.

All: **Our Father, . . .**

Minister: God of goodness and love,
hear our prayers for the sick members of our community
and for all who are in need.

Amid mental and physical suffering
may they find consolation in your healing presence.
Show your mercy as you close wounds, cure illness,
make broken bodies whole and free downcast spirits.
May these special people find lasting health and deliverance,
and join us in thanksgiving for all your gifts.

We ask this through the Lord Jesus
who healed those who believed.

All: **Amen.**

All may share refreshments.

Concluding Rite

Minister: [We] will extol you, O [our] God and King,
and [we] will bless your name forever and ever.

Ps 145:1

All: **Every day will [we] bless you,
and [we] will praise your name forever and ever.**

Ps 145:2

Closing Song: **Make Us True Servants** or any suitable song.

Home Service—
The Christian Family

Introductory Rites

Opening Song: **Make Us True Servants** or any suitable song.

Call to Celebration

Leader: In the name of the Father, and of the Son and of the Holy Spirit.

All: **Amen.**

Leader: With three things I am delighted,
    for they are pleasing to the LORD and to men:
 Harmony among brethren, friendship among neighbors,
    and the mutual love of husband and wife.   Sir 25:1

All: **If we love one another, God remains in us,
 and his love is brought to perfection in us.**   1 Jn 4:12

Opening Prayer

Leader: Let us pray.

 Jesus, you are with us now.
 May we be strengthened in our love
 and in our appreciation of one another.
 We desire to bring the light of faith
 to the people in our neighborhood, schools and places of work,
 especially to those who find life meaningless
 because they are without faith, hope or love.

 We pray in your holy name.

All: **Amen.**

Reading of the Word of God

Select one of the following readings.

Romans 2:1-2, 9-18 (L775-2)
 [Renew your mind so that you may judge what is good, pleasing and perfect.]

Ephesians 4:30 — 5:2 (L812-4)

[Follow Christ's way of love and be mutually forgiving.]

Colossians 3:12-17 (L775-6)

[Above all, have love, the bond of perfection.]

Response

Leader: We will pause to talk and pray about Paul's counsels on the Christian life.

All discuss their role in the family in light of the reading and meditation.

Song: **Whatsoever You Do** or **Where Charity and Love Prevail** or any suitable song.

Action

The family may choose a sign of their resolution to help one another live Jesus' way. It may be a specially decorated candle to be lit at meals and special occasions such as birthdays, anniversaries and holy days. It may be a religious picture, the Bible enthroned, or another significant object.

Leader: To show our intention to be faithful, let us join hands for the Lord's Prayer.

All: **Our Father, . . .**

Before concluding, the family may share a treat, celebrating their joy in one another.

Concluding Rite

Leader: May the grace of our Lord Jesus Christ be with us always.

All: **Forever and ever. Amen.**

Closing Song: **We Bring His Holy Love** or a favorite family song.

Prayer Service—Peace

Introductory Rites

Commentator: Experiencing conflict, discord and struggle, we say with
Jeremiah: " 'Peace, peace!' . . . though there is no peace"
(6:14). This service seeks to show that sin frustrates God's
plan for peace. We may begin to realize peace when we try
to accomplish what Dante said long ago: "In his will is our
peace." In that spirit we pray: "O God, let there be peace,
and let it begin with me."

Opening Song: **Let There Be Peace on Earth** or any suitable song.

Call to Worship

Minister: Blest are the peacemakers;
for they will be called children of God.   Mt 5:9

All: **Lord, make me an instrument of your peace.**

Opening Prayer

Minister: Let us pray.

Jesus, Prince of peace,
our lives are torn by war,
our own private battles and great world conflicts.
Our presence here shows our desire to be peaceful people.
Strengthen our efforts to live in harmony,
loving one another in peace.

We ask this through Christ our Lord.

All: **Amen.**

Reading of the Word of God

First Reading: Isaiah 2:1-5 (L816-1)
[Promise of Peace]

Response: Psalm 122:6-8

All: **Pray for the peace of Jerusalem!**
            May those who love you prosper!
            May peace be within your walls,
            prosperity in your buildings.
            Because of my relatives and friends
            I will say, "Peace be within you!"

Second Reading: Philippians 4:6-9 (L832-1)
    [Conditions for Peace]

Response: **Peace for Our Times** or any suitable song.

Homily

Resolution

Minister: Peace I leave with you;
             my peace I give to you.   Jn 14:27

All: **Lord, make me an instrument of your peace.**

Minister: Do not be conquered by evil
             but conquer evil with good.   Rom 12:21

All: **Where there is hatred, let me sow love.**

Minister: Father, forgive them;
             they know not what they do.   Lk 23:34

All: **Where there is injury, let me sow pardon.**

Minister: Do not be unbelieving, but believe.   Jn 20:27

All: **Where there is doubt, let me sow faith.**

Minister: Hope does not disappoint,
             because the love of God has been poured out into our hearts
             through the Holy Spirit that has been given to us.   Rom 5:5

All: **Where there is despair, let me sow hope.**

Minister: You are the light of the world.
             Your light must shine before others,
             that they may see your good deeds and glorify your heavenly
             Father.   Mt 5:14, 16

All: **Where there is darkness, let me sow light.**

Minister: You will weep and mourn, while the world rejoices;
you will grieve,
but your grief will become joy. Jn 16:20

All: **Where there is sadness, let me sow joy.**

Minister: [God] encourages us in our every affliction,
so that we may be able to encourage those who are in any
affliction with the encouragement with which we ourselves have
received from him. 2 Cor 1:4

All: **Divine Master, grant that I may not**
so much seek to be consoled as to console.

Minister: In all wisdom and insight, he has made known to us the mystery
of his will in accord with his favor that he set forth in him.
Eph 1:8-9

All: **Grant that I may not so much seek**
to be understood as to understand.

Minister: If I speak in human and angelic tongues,
but do not have love,
I am a resounding gong or a clashing cymbal. 1 Cor 13:1

All: **Grant that I may not so much seek**
to be loved as to love.

Minister: Whoever wishes to save his life will lose it,
but whoever loses his life for my sake will save it. Lk 9:24

All: **It is in giving that we receive.**

Minister: Forgive us our debts
as we forgive our debtors. Mt 6:12

All: **It is in pardoning that we are pardoned.**

Minister: Unless a grain of wheat falls to the ground and dies, it remains
just a grain of wheat;
but if it dies, it produces much fruit. Jn 12:24

All: **It is in dying that we are born to eternal life.**

Concluding Rite

Blessing

Minister: May God the Father and the Lord Jesus Christ
grant us peace and love and faith.

All: **Grace be with all
who love our Lord Jesus Christ with unfailing love.**

Closing Song: **Prayer of Saint Francis** or any suitable song.

SERVICE FOR CHRISTIAN UNITY

Introductory Rites

Opening Song: **There Is One Lord** or **In My Name** or any suitable song.

Call to Prayer

Minister: Come, let us return to the LORD, . . .
he will heal us, . . . he will bind our wounds. Hos 6:1

All: **[Let us] look to him [and] be radiant with joy,
[that our] faces may not blush with shame.** Ps 34:6

Opening Prayer

Minister: Let us express our faith as we pray the words
handed down to us through Christian tradition as the Apostles'
Creed.

All: **I believe in God, the Father almighty,
creator of heaven and earth.
I believe in Jesus Christ, his only Son, our Lord.
He was conceived by the power of the Holy Spirit
and born of the Virgin Mary.
He suffered under Pontius Pilate,
was crucified, died, and was buried.
He descended to the dead.
On the third day he rose again.
He ascended into heaven,
and is seated at the right hand of the Father.
He will come again to judge the living and the dead.
I believe in the Holy Spirit,
the holy catholic Church,
the communion of saints,
the forgiveness of sins,
the resurrection of the body,
and the life everlasting. Amen.**

Reading of the Word of God

First Reading: Leviticus 26:3-6, 9, 11-12 (adapted)
[The Lord will care for his people.]

Reader: A reading from the book of Leviticus.

If you live in accordance with my precepts and are careful to follow my directions, I will give you rain so that the crops grow and you have enough food to eat. I will bring peace that you may sleep without fear. I will love you and keep my promises to you. I will be with you because I am your God and you are my people.

This is the Word of the Lord. **Thanks be to God.**

Response: **All You Nations** or **The King of Love** or any suitable song.

Second Reading: Ephesians 2:19-22 (L812-2)

[We are the Lord's temple.]

Response: **The Church's One Foundation** or any suitable song.

Gospel: John 10:11-16 (L815-3)

[There shall be one flock, one shepherd.]

Homily

Intercessions

(based on Eph 4:5-6, 31-32)

Minister: Hope for Christian unity begins with respect for one another. Let us pray for peace and harmony among all people.

All: **Father, may those divided by anger, fear or misunderstanding see the truth and forgive one another.**

Minister: Let us pray for Christian unity.

All: **May we see the blessings of variety in our traditions and find unity in one Lord, one faith, one baptism, one God and Father.**

We may add other intentions at this point with the response:

All: **Lord, hear our prayer.**

Minister: Let us pray in the words our Savior taught us:

All: **Our Father, . . .**

Concluding Rite

Blessing

Minister: May the God of endurance and encouragement
grant you to think in harmony with one another
in keeping with Christ Jesus,
that with one accord you may with one voice
glorify God, the Father of our Lord Jesus Christ.

Rom 15:5-6

All: **Amen.**

Closing Song: **Where Charity and Love Prevail** or **Christ Is Our Peace!** or any
suitable song.

Behold Your Mother—
May Crowning Service

Introductory Rites

Commentator: Born of earth yet called from heaven, Mary said ''Yes'' to God. She gave birth to the Savior, raised him to greatness, and stood helpless as he died on the cross. Risen in glory, Jesus shares her with us. Beholding our Mother's strength, we too can say ''Yes'' to God.

Opening Song: **O Most Holy One** or any suitable song.

Opening Prayer

Minister: In the name of the Father, and of the Son, and of the Holy Spirit.

All: **Amen.**

Minister: Let us pray.

> Almighty God,
> life is your most sacred gift.
> You implanted divine life in Mary
> and she gave birth to the Savior of the world.
> You share divine life with each of us
> and ask us to share your saving love with all we meet.
> May we join Mary and say ''Yes''
> to all that you call us to be and do.
>
> We ask this through Christ our Lord.

All: **Amen.**

Reading of the Word of God

First Reading: The United States Bishops, ''Behold Your Mother'' (nos. 8-9)

[Mary Our Mother]

Reader: A reading from the Bishops' Pastoral Letter ''Behold Your Mother.''

We honor Mary as the Mother of Jesus Christ, the Incarnate Word of

God. We recognize her unique and exalted role in the redemption her Son brought us. We love Mary. We try to imitate her virtues of faith, purity, humility and conformity to the will of God, which are part of the very texture of the gospel message. We acknowledge that devotion to Mary, the joyful duty of all of us, has a special function in exalting the dignity of woman and fostering respect for her person. We believe in the power of Mary's intercession to bring us, as individuals and as a community, under the influence of Jesus' redeeming mercy.

Here ends the reading. **Thanks be to God.**

Response: **Daily, Daily Sing to Mary** or any suitable song.

Gospel: John 19:26-27
[Mary is Jesus' gift to us.]

Response:

Minister: Mary gives us Jesus, the light of the world.

All: **May he shine forth through us.**

Minister: Mary gives us Jesus crucified.

All: **May we die to our selfish inclinations.**

Minister: Mary gives us Jesus, risen to new life.

All: **May we rise through our life to eternal glory.**

Homily

Song: **Hail, Holy Queen Enthroned Above** or any suitable song.

The crowning may occur during the song.

Litany of Mary, Mother of the Church

This optional litany springs partially from terminology in the Bishops' Pastoral Letter. The traditional litany may be substituted.

Minister:	*All:*
Lord, have mercy.	**Lord, have mercy.**
Christ, have mercy.	**Christ, have mercy.**

Lord, have mercy.	**Lord, have mercy.**
God our Father in heaven,	**have mercy on us.**
God the Son, our Redeemer,	**have mercy on us.**
God the Holy Spirit,	**have mercy on us.**
Holy Trinity, one God,	**have mercy on us.**
Holy Mary,	**pray for us.**
Mother of God,	**pray for us.**
Woman of faith,	**pray for us.**
Most honored of all virgins,	**pray for us.**
Joy of Israel,	**pray for us.**
Honor of our people,	**pray for us.**
Model of prayer and virtue,	**pray for us.**
Incentive to trust,	**pray for us.**
Temple of the Holy Spirit,	**pray for us.**
Spouse of Joseph,	**pray for us.**
Mother of Jesus,	**pray for us.**
Faithful follower of Jesus,	**pray for us.**
Mother of the church,	**pray for us.**
Image of the church at prayer,	**pray for us.**
Our Lady of Guadalupe, patroness of the Americas,	**pray for us.**
Mary Immaculate, patroness of the United States,	**pray for us.**
Advocate of life,	**pray for us.**
Guide for the young,	**pray for us.**
Friend of the single,	**pray for us.**
Companion of the married,	**pray for us.**
Voice for the unborn,	**pray for us.**
Mother of mothers,	**pray for us.**
Support of the family,	**pray for us.**
Comforter of the sick,	**pray for us.**
Nurse of the aged,	**pray for us.**
Echo of the suffering,	**pray for us.**
Consoler of the widowed,	**pray for us.**
Strength of the brokenhearted,	**pray for us.**

Hymn of the joyful,	**pray for us.**
Hope of the poor,	**pray for us.**
Example of detachment for the rich,	**pray for us.**
Goal of pilgrims,	**pray for us.**
Resort of the traveler,	**pray for us.**
Protector of the exile,	**pray for us.**
Woman most whole,	**pray for us.**
Virgin most free,	**pray for us.**
Wife most loving,	**pray for us.**
Mother most fulfilled,	**pray for us.**
Queen of love,	**pray for us.**
Lamb of God, you take away the sins of the world:	**have mercy on us.**
Lamb of God, you take away the sins of the world:	**have mercy on us.**
Lamb of God, you take away the sins of the world:	**have mercy on us.**

All: **Remember, O most loving Virgin Mary,
that never was it known
that anyone who fled to your protection,
implored your help, or sought your intercession
was left unaided.
Inspired with this confidence, we turn to you,
O Virgin of virgins, our Mother.
To you we come, before you we stand,
sinful and sorrowful.
O Mother of the Word Incarnate,
do not despise our petitions,
but in your mercy hear and answer us.
Amen.**

Concluding Rite

(based on the Bishop's Pastoral Letter, no. 146)

Minister: May Mary's pilgrimage of faith strengthen us
in our individual Christian vocations.

All: **Amen.**

Minister: May Mary's loving desire that her Son's words be heeded hasten Christian unity.

All: **Amen.**

Minister: May Mary's motherly intercession
make us worthy of Jesus' promises.

All: **Amen.**

Minister: Mary is the daughter of God the Father,
Spouse of God the Holy Spirit
and Mother of God the Son.
May the blessing of the Holy Trinity
come upon us and remain with us for ever.

All: **Amen.**

Closing Song: **One in Joyful Songs of Praise** or any suitable song.

The Gift of Beauty in the Land—
Scripture Service

We celebrate our blessings and pray that all people may protect these gifts from needless, selfish destruction. This service may be celebrated outdoors in a place of natural beauty.

Introductory Rites

Opening Song: **America the Beautiful** or any suitable song.

Call to Celebration

Minister: Open your eyes, your hearts, your whole selves, and sense the good things we have from the Lord our God.

All: **Bless the LORD for all he has done!**   Sir 39:14

Opening Prayer

Minister: Let us pray.

Creator of the universe, we are your people.
You bless our earth with natural beauty and wealth.
Show us the way to use these blessings without destroying them.
Increase our appreciation of clean air, pure water
and the breathtaking beauty of the natural landscape.
May our lifetime here enable others to have
such blessings in future generations.

We ask this in your holy name.

All: **Amen.**

Reading of the Word of God

Reading: Deuteronomy 8:7-14, 20 (adapted)
[Praise God for his blessings.]

Reader: A reading from the book of Deuteronomy.

The Lord, our God, provides for us a good country: a land with streams of water, with springs and fountains welling up in the hills and valleys, a land of wheat and barley, of vines, fruit trees and vegetables, of shade trees and of honey, a land where we can eat bread without restriction and where we lack nothing, a land whose stones contain iron and in whose hills we can mine copper. But when we have eaten our fill, we must bless the Lord, our God, for the good country he has given us. Be careful not to forget the Lord, our God, by neglecting his decrees, statutes and natural laws: lest, when we have eaten our fill, and have built fine houses and lived in them, and have increased our herds and flocks, our silver and gold, and all our property and wealth, we then become haughty of heart and unmindful of the Lord, our God. Not heeding the voice of the Lord, we shall perish.

This is the Word of the Lord. **Thanks be to God.**

Litany of Praise and Thanksgiving

(In style of Daniel 3:52-90)

Minister: Blest are you, O Lord, the God of creation.
Praiseworthy and exalted forever.

Blest are you, Lord of all nations.
Praiseworthy and exalted forever.

Bless the Lord, all you works of the Lord.
Praise and exalt God forever.

Northern lights and sunny days, bless the Lord.
Praise and exalt God forever.

Twinkling stars and darkest night, bless the Lord.
Praise and exalt God forever.

Sky and clouds and heaven above, bless the Lord.
Praise and exalt God forever.

Dew and fog and glistening frost, bless the Lord.

Praise and exalt God forever.

All you winds, bless the Lord.
Praise and exalt God forever.

All you seasons, bless the Lord.
Praise and exalt God forever.

Tundra and deserts, fields and plains, bless the Lord.
Praise and exalt God forever.

All mountains and hills, bless the Lord.
Praise and exalt God forever.

All lakes and ponds, bless the Lord.
Praise and exalt God forever.

All rivers and streams, bless the Lord.
Praise and exalt God forever.

Hot springs, geysers and fountains, bless the Lord.
Praise and exalt God forever.

Coal mines, gold and silver mines, gravel pits and oil wells, bless the Lord.
Praise and exalt God forever.

All you animals wild and tame, bless the Lord.
Praise and exalt God forever.

All you birds of the air, bless the Lord.
Praise and exalt God forever.

All you fish in the shallows and depths, bless the Lord.
Praise and exalt God forever.

All you natural resources and wealth of this land, bless the Lord.
Praise and exalt God forever.

All you commerce and industry, business and trade, bless the Lord.
Praise and exalt God forever.

Church bells, school bells and cow bells, bless the Lord.

Praise and exalt God forever.

Cities and towns, suburbs, farms and ranches, bless the Lord.

Praise and exalt God forever.

Automobiles and trains, airplanes and ships, bless the Lord.

Praise and exalt God forever.

Bicycles, scooters and wagons, all moving things, bless the Lord.

Praise and exalt God forever.

Train whistles, factory whistles and all whistles, bless the Lord.

Praise and exalt God forever.

Skyscrapers and hotels, hogans and teepees, bungalows and apartments, bless the Lord.

Praise and exalt God forever.

Citizens of this land, bless the Lord.

Praise and exalt God forever.

A talk or discussion may follow this litany. Participants could prepare slides or other presentations. These activities may initiate and stimulate local ecological programs.

Concluding Rite

Minister: Filled with God's praises,
we return home glorifying him.
May peace be with us all, now and forever.

All: **Amen.**

Closing Song: **Bless This Bounteous Land of Freedom** or **Lord of Nations, God Eternal** or any suitable song.

Prayer Service Before Elections

Introductory Rites

Opening Song: **Lord of Nations, God Eternal** or **Bless This Bounteous Land of Freedom** or any suitable song.

Greeting

Minister: Grace to you and peace
from him who is and who was and who is to come.   Rv 1:4

All: **The ruler of the kings of earth.**   Rv 1:5

Call to Worship

Minister: O God, open our eyes.

All: **That we may see the way of truth.**

Minister: O Lord, keep us from all selfish intent.

All: **And hear us when we call on you.**

Opening Prayer

Minister: Let us pray.

> All-knowing God,
> we gather to hear your word
> and to pray for your guidance as we approach the time
> to elect those who will next serve the nation in public office.
> Enlighten our minds with understanding and perception
> that we may continue to discover your truth.
> Endow our wills with the strength to strive for justice.
> Fill our hearts with love for the peace you alone give,
> that we may be at peace with one another.
> May our individual lives serve the good
> of all the people of our land and beyond its shores.
>
> We ask this through Christ our Lord.

All: **Amen.**

Reading of the Word of God

First Reading: Exodus 18:20-22, 24; Deuteronomy 1:13-14, 16-17
(adapted)

[Choose those who are wise, trustworthy and honest.]

Reader: A reading from the books of Exodus and Deuteronomy.

Jethro said to his son-in-law Moses: "Enlighten the people, showing them how they are to live. But you should also look for able and God-fearing men, trustworthy men who hate dishonest gain. Let these men render decisions for the people." Moses followed the advice of his father-in-law.

Then he spoke to the people: "Choose wise, intelligent and experienced men from your tribes, that I may appoint them as your leaders." They answered, "We agree to do as you have proposed."

Moses charged the judges: "Listen to complaints and administer true justice to both parties, even if one is an alien. In rendering judgment, do not consider who a person is; give ear to the lowly and to the great alike, fearing no man, for judgment is God's."

This is the word of the Lord.   **Thanks be to God.**

Response: Psalm 72:1-2, 3-4ab, 7-8, 12-13, 17 (L833)

R. Justice shall flourish in his time and fullness of peace forever.

Second Reading: 2 Chronicles 19:5-7; 9-10 (adapted)

[Because you judge on the Lord's behalf, act carefully and faithfully.]

Reader: A reading from the second book of Chronicles.

King Jehosaphat appointed judges and said to them: "Take care what you do, for you are judging on behalf of the Lord; he judges with you. Act carefully, for with the Lord there is no injustice, no partiality, no bribe-taking. You shall act faithfully in the fear of the Lord. In every dispute that your brethren bring to you, whether it concerns bloodguilt or questions of law or judgments, warn them lest they become guilty before the Lord and his wrath come upon you and your brethren."

This is the word of the Lord.   **Thanks be to God.**

Homily

Intercessions

Minister: We conclude our service with prayer for God's help.

Reader: That love for justice may prevail in our elections,
we pray to the Lord.

R. Lord, hear us and lead us to justice.

That all voters may exercise their right to vote,
we pray to the Lord. **R.**

That the news media may report the complete truth,
we pray to the Lord. **R.**

That election judges and poll watchers may be honest,
we pray to the Lord. **R.**

For wisdom and courage in elected officials,
we pray to the Lord. **R.**

For peace and justice, at home and abroad,
we pray to the Lord. **R.**

Other intentions may be added.

Minister: Lord of all, both governed and governing,
let us love all that is just and life-giving.
Instill in us the desire for your glory
and the well-being of all people.
Help us in our deliberations
to find candidates of honor and integrity.
May our leaders, judges and all public servants
be worthy stewards of peace and freedom.

We ask this through Christ our Lord.

All: **Amen.**

Conclusion

Minister: The peace of God be with us.
May he guide our deliberations with his light
as we decide on suitable representatives in government.

All: **Thanks be to God.**

Closing Song: **America the Beautiful** or **God Bless Our Native Land** or any suitable song.

Independence Day Celebration

Introductory Rites

Opening Song: **Lord of Nations, God Eternal** or any suitable song.

Throughout the program, a master of ceremonies may introduce the minister(s), reader(s), speaker(s) and other participants and public figures.

Opening Prayer

Minister: Let us pray.

> Almighty, everlasting God, the Ruler of all nations,
> hear us as we gather around our flag
> to celebrate liberty and justice for all.
> May it remind us of the love
> we owe to our country and all our fellow citizens,
> of fidelity to our national ideals,
> and of the desired unity of all people.
> When we see our flag stand out in the breeze,
> may it move our hearts to rededication to the common good.
> May we always walk worthy of the ideals
> of our colors and our country.
>
> We pray in your holy name.

All: **Amen.**

Reading of the Word of God

First Reading: Psalm 8:2, 4-10
  [The Lord is exalted above all creation.]

Response: **America the Beautiful** or **Stewards of Earth** or any suitable song.

Second Reading: Is 32:15b-18
  [Interdependence of Peace, Justice and Liberty]

Response: Abraham Lincoln, Second Inaugural Address

Minister: With malice toward none, with charity for all —

R. The fruit of righteousness is sown in peace. Jas 3:18

With firmness in the right, as God gives us to see the right—**R.**

Let us strive to finish the work we are in,
to bind up the nation's wounds—**R.**

To care for him who shall have borne the battle
and his widow and orphan—**R.**

To do all which may achieve and cherish a just and lasting peace
among ourselves and with all nations—**R.**

A public leader may address the assembly. In lieu of an address there may be some other manifestation of civic pride, such as a fireworks display where authorized, a patriotic musical performance, an artillery salute, or the raising or posting of the flag.

Resolution

Minister: Will you foster peace within our country
and good will among all people?

All: **We will.**

Minister: Will you stand up for justice by keeping our laws
and fulfilling the divine law of love?

All: **We will.**

Minister: Will you labor to enrich our land with your God-given talents,
curing its ills and respecting its life in all its forms?

All: **We will.**

Litany of Petition

Minister: Let us pray for our country,
that it may be a blessing to the world:

R. Lord, hear our prayer.

Let us pray for our president, the members of Congress, our
governor and all who serve us in public office: **R.**

Let us pray for sound government and just laws,
good education and justice at all levels of society: **R.**

Let us pray for all the citizens of our country,
for the removal of all hatred, prejudice and contempt
for those not of our color, class or creed: **R.**

Let us pray for peace and understanding among all people,
for the day when war will be no more and all will be
truly free in their human dignity and rights: **R.**

Let us pray for all those who serve us,
especially in the search for ways to better the quality of life: **R.**

Let us pray for the proper use of freedom,
especially in using our natural resources: **R.**

Concluding Rite

Closing Prayer

Minister: Let us pray.

Heavenly Father,
you have given us this good land for our heritage.
Enlighten us, that we may always provide a haven
for all who seek freedom and justice.
Defend our liberties and fashion into one united people
the multitude brought here at different times
out of many nations and tongues.
Sustain us as we strive today to renew the freedoms
achieved at so great a price.
As we work to harness nature's resources for the good of all,
keep us from violence and discord, pride and arrogance.
Guide us along the path of justice
which righteous, honorable men and women have walked
before us.

We ask this in your name, God forever and ever.

All: **Amen.**

Dimissal

Minister: May the LORD, our God, be with us
as he was with our fathers
and may he not forsake us nor cast us off.   1 Kgs 8:57

All: **May he draw our hearts to himself,**
that we may follow him in everything
and keep the commands, statutes and ordinances
which he enjoined on our fathers.   1 Kgs 8:58

Minister: Go forth in peace and freedom, renewed in spirit
to make our promised land of yesteryear
a true home for today and a sanctuary for all future generations.

All: **Amen.**

Closing Song: **America** or any suitable song.

PENITENTIAL SERVICES

A New Beginning— Penitential Service

Introductory Rites

With special New Year rites, ancient people endeavored to abolish the past, so that there could be a new birth of times. After rites of purification, confession of sin and exorcism, the people entered another cycle of time. They were refreshed and reborn in spirit. In our time, New Year's resolutions reflect these efforts to make things new. This is a new year. Before much of it slips into the past, we take time to consider this new beginning.

Opening Song: **We Are the Light of the World** or any suitable song.

Call to a New Beginning

Minister: We were once darkness.

All: **Now [we] are light in the Lord.**

Minister: Light produces every kind of goodness and righteousness and truth.

All: **Let us live as people of light.**   Eph 5:8-9

Opening Prayer

Minister: Let us pray.

Almighty Father,
when time began you were the Lord of that moment.
As this new year advances, you are Lord of each moment.
May you who stand at the beginning of time and beyond it guide us in our use of time during this year.

We ask this through Christ our Lord.

All: **Amen.**

Reading of the Word of God

First Reading: Hosea 6:1-3
   [The Lord revives us, if we return to him.]

Response:

Minister:	All:
Creative love of the Father,	**Renew the face of the earth.**
Jesus among us,	**Renew the face of the earth.**
Continuing guidance of the Holy Spirit,	**Renew the face of the earth.**
Caring for one another,	**We are people of light.**
With sacrifices throughout the year,	**We are people of light.**
Giving food to the hungry and drink to the thirsty,	**We are people of light.**
Clothing the naked and sheltering the homeless,	**We are people of light.**
Visiting the imprisoned and the sick,	**We are people of light.**
Burying the dead,	**We are people of light.**
Shedding our selfishness and sin,	**We are people of light.**
Forgiving one another,	**We are people of light.**

Gospel: Luke 13:6-9

   [Jesus expects us to bear good fruit.]

Reflection

Pause for reflection after each thought. The minister may also offer a brief homily based on these ideas.

The signs of life I give to others are . . .

My tree of life bears fruit when . . .

Jesus' light shines through me when . . .

For the New Year I will try . . .

Resolution

All: **God our Father, we worship you**
as our first beginning, our constant help and protection,
and the source of our lasting happiness.
With your widsom, guide us through this New Year.
May we courageously accept all its duties
and advance through all it holds for us.
Help us to rise above our human weaknesses,
that we may forgive the wrongs against us
as you forgive us our offenses.
Let us forget ourselves
and reach out to others in peace and love.
Father, may we be one with you forever,
through Jesus, the Lord. Amen.

Concluding Rite

Closing Prayer

Minister: Let us pray.

Almighty Father, a new year has dawned over the earth,
and we pray for your gift of peace.
Grant that the joy that fills our hearts during this season
may bring harmony to our homes and places of work.
Let your Son's light shine on our world's uncertainties.
May all of us come to live with you forever.

We ask this through Christ our Lord.

All: **Amen.**

Blessing

Minister: May the almighty Lord order our days and deeds in his peace,
and lead us to everlasting life.

All: **Amen.**

Closing Song: **Let There Be Peace on Earth** or **Peace for Our Times** or any
suitable song.

RESPECT FOR LIFE—
PENITENTIAL SERVICE

Introductory Rites

Opening Song: **I Lift My Heart** or any suitable song.

Call to Worship

Minister: Blessed be the God and Father of our Lord Jesus Christ, who in his great mercy gave us a new birth to a living hope through the resurrection of Jesus Christ from the dead.   1 Pt 1:3

All: **In him we live and move and have our being.**   Acts 17:28

Opening Prayer

Minister: Let us pray.

O God, our eyes behold the beauty of your creation,
and our ears catch the sounds of your power.
We hold our lives sacred because they are your gift.
Bring us to greater awareness of the sanctity of human life
and to sorrow for the times we have ignored or offended it.

We ask this through Christ our Lord.

All: **Amen.**

Reading of the Word of God

First Reading: Pope John XXIII, "Peace on Earth," nos. 9, 11, 29-30
[The Basis of Respect for Life]

Reader: A reading from the encyclical letter, "Peace on Earth."

Human society, to be well-ordered and productive, must lay down as a foundation the principle that every human being is a person whose nature is endowed with intelligence and free will. Flowing directly and simultaneously from this nature are rights and obligations which are universal and inviolable, and which cannot be surrendered in any way. The rights of persons include the right to life, to bodily integrity, and to the means which are necessary and suitable for the proper development of life and its secure maintenance.

The right of every person to life is correlative with the duty to preserve it; the right to a decent manner of living with the duty of living it becomingly. It is also clear that, in human society, to every person's right there corresponds a duty in all other persons to acknowledge and respect the right in question. Since we are social by nature, we are meant to live with others and to work for one another's well-being. A well-ordered society requires that we recognize and observe our mutual rights and duties. It also demands that each contribute generously to the establishment of a civic order in which rights and duties are sincerely and effectively acknowledged and fulfilled.

Here ends the reading. **Thanks be to God.**

Response: Psalm 27:1, 13

All: **The LORD is my light and my salvation;**
whom should I fear?
The LORD is my life's refuge;
of whom should I be afraid?
I believe that I shall see the bounty of the LORD
in the land of the living.

Second Reading: Deuteronomy 30:15-20 (L752-4)
[Our Call to Respect Life]

Response: **Choose Life!** or any suitable song.

Gospel: Matthew 25:31-40
[The Way to Respect Life]

Homily

Intercessions

Minister: All life comes from the Father.
With lively faith we ask his blessing on the living.

Reader: For a greater realization of the sanctity of marriage,
that parents may be conscious of their calling
as they share in God's creative power,
we pray to the Lord.

R.   For life we pray.

For governments and all civil legislators,
that they may enact laws
that uphold God's fundamental law
and every person's right to life,
we pray to the Lord.   **R.**

For those who have acted against human life,
that they may know the wrong
and experience forgiveness,
we pray to the Lord.   **R.**

For those whose lives are threatened by illness or accident,
for those responsible for preserving the sacredness of life,
and for ourselves, that we may have greater concern for all,
we pray to the Lord.   **R.**

That young people may respect life and love,
that the elderly may be thankful for their many years,
and that all may live lives pleasing to God,
we pray to the Lord.   **R.**

Concluding Rite

All: **God our Father,**
you showed us how much we mean to you
when you sent Jesus, your Son, into our world.
He died for us to demonstrate your love.
We pray that we may heed the lessons of his life
and today's lessons in all life's encounters.
May our respect for one another increase.
When we improve the quality of life,
let it be for all, not just for those we know.
We ask this through Jesus who lives forever. Amen.

Blessing

Minister: May God the Creator
bless and guide us in the way of righteousness.

All: **Amen.**

Minister: May God the Redeemer
teach us respect for the sanctity of life
and lead us to eternal life.

All: **Amen.**

Minister: May God the Sanctifier
strengthen our wills to uphold faithfully
each person's right to life.

All: **Amen.**

A priest or deacon adds:

May almighty God bless you,
the Father, and the Son, and the Holy Spirit.

All: **Amen.**

Closing Song: **Now Thank We All Our God** or any suitable song.

Heart for Hearts— Penitential Service

Introductory Rites

Commentator: God's first covenant with his people was given to Moses on two stone tablets. In refusing to live within this relationship, the people cultivated what the prophets called a "hardness of heart." The people's hearts seemed made of the same stone as the Law.

The new covenant was to be written in the heart, replacing our stony hearts with natural ones. To speak to our stony hearts, God reveals his love through Jesus. Jesus' pierced heart moves us to recognize the malice of sin and the goodness of salvation.

This service develops the theme of the two covenants. It is clearly a case of "heart for hearts." God writes a new covenant. Our response will allow it to increase within us because we have a change of heart.

Opening Song: **You Shall Be My People** or any suitable song.

Call to Worship

Minister: The sin of Judah is written
    with an iron stylus,
  Engraved with a diamond point
    upon the tablets of their hearts.   Jer 17:1

All: **Those who fear the LORD prepare their hearts
and humble themselves before him.**   Sir 2:17

Reading of the Word of God

First Reading: Jeremiah 31:31-34 (35-B)
  [Promise of a New Heart]

Response:

Minister: I will give you a new heart
    and place a new spirit within you,

taking from your bodies your stony hearts
and giving you natural hearts.   Ez 36:26

**R.   A clean heart create for me, O God,
        and a steadfast spirt renew within me.**

                                                             Ps 51:12

Yet even now, says the LORD, return to me with your whole
heart,
with fasting, and weeping, and mourning.   **R.**   Jl 2:12

I will give [you] a heart with which to understand
that I am the LORD.
[You] shall be my people and I will be [your] God,
for [you] shall return to me with [your] whole heart.   **R.**   Jer 24:7

Oh, that today you would hear his voice:
"Harden not your hearts."   **R.**   Ps 95:7-8

Gospel: John 19:31-35 (L761-12)
        [Jesus' Heart]

Homily

Resolution

Commentator: Just as the Ten Commandments constituted the charter of
the old covenant, so the Beatitudes mark the charter of the
new. The Beatitudes are presented in the light of their
background in the Hebrew Scriptures, emphasizing that the
new is hidden in the old, and the old is made manifest in
the new.

Minister: The lowly will ever find joy in the LORD,
        and the poor rejoice in the Holy One of Israel.

                                                             Is 29:19

All: **Blessed are the poor in spirit,
        for theirs is the kingdom of heaven.**   Mt 5:3

Minister: The Lord GOD will wipe away
        the tears from all faces.   Is 25:8

All: **Blessed are they who mourn,
        for they will be comforted.**   Mt 5:4

Minister: The meek shall possess the land,
        they shall delight in abounding peace.   Ps 37:11

All:	**Blessed are the meek, for they will inherit the land.**	Mt 5:5
Minister:	The LORD said to Moses, ''Speak to the . . . community and tell them: Be holy, for I, the LORD, your God, am holy.''	
		Lv 19:1-2
All:	**Blessed are they who hunger and thirst for righteousness, for they will be satisfied.**	Mt 5:6
Minister:	A kindly man benefits himself, but a merciless man harms himself.	Prv 11:17
All:	**Blessed are the merciful, for they will be shown mercy.**	Mt 5:7
Minister:	From my flesh I shall see God; my inmost being is consumed with longing.	
		Job 19:26
All:	**Blessed are the clean of heart, for they will see God.**	Mt 5:8
Minister:	Watch the wholehearted man, and mark the upright; for there is a future for the man of peace.	
		Ps 37:37
All:	**Blessed are the peacemakers; for they will be called children of God.**	Mt 5:9
Minister:	The LORD is close to the broken-hearted; and those who are crushed in spirit he saves.	
		Ps 34:19
All:	**Blessed are they who are persecuted for the sake of righteousness, for theirs is the kingdom of God.**	Mt 5:10
Minister:	For your sake I bear insult, and shame covers my face.	Ps 69:8
All:	**Blessed are you when they insult you and persecute you and utter every kind of evil against you [falsely] because of me.**	Mt 5:11

Concluding Rite

Minister:	Thus says the LORD: It is I who wipe out your offenses; your sins I remember no more.	Is 43:25

All: **God who is rich in mercy,**
            because of the great love he had for us
            even when we were dead in our transgressions,
            brought us to life with Christ.   Eph 2:4-5

Dismissal

Minister: Let us go forth in peace.

All: **Thanks be to God.**

Closing Song: **We Are the Light of the World** or any suitable song.

CHRISTIAN JOY—
PENITENTIAL SERVICE

Introductory Rites

Opening Song: **Joyful, Joyful, We Adore Thee** or any suitable song.

Call to Celebration   (Phil 4:4-7, adapted)

Minister: Rejoice in the Lord always!

All: **Indeed, let us rejoice!**

Minister: The Lord is near.

All: **Let us dismiss all anxiety from our minds.**

Minister: Present your needs to God in grateful prayer.

All: **May his peace stand guard in our hearts and minds.**

Opening Prayer

Minister: Let us ask the Father for the gift of joy.

Father,
send forth your Spirit of light,
that we may understand our conversion
from sin as a new departure,
a setting out,
an advancement in true freedom and joy.
May the Spirit pour joy into our hearts
as we reflect on
and experience your forgiveness.

We ask this through Christ our Lord.

All: **Amen.**

Reading of the Word of God

First Reading: Pope Paul VI, *Christian Joy*, May 9, 1975
[Every heart needs joy.]

Reader: A reading from the *Apostolic Exhortation on Christian Joy*.

There is need to savor in a simple way the many human joys that the Creator places in our path: the elating joy of existence and of life; the joy of chaste and sanctified love; the peaceful joy of nature and silence; the sometimes austere joy of work well done; the joy and satisfaction of duty performed; the transparent joy of purity, service and sharing; the demanding joy of sacrifice. These natural joys were often used by Jesus as a starting-point when he proclaimed the kingdom of God.

Here ends the reading.   **Thanks be to God.**

Response: **Rejoice in the Lord** or any suitable song.

Second Reading: Pope Paul VI, *Christian Joy*, May 9, 1975
[Joy is a fruit of creative love.]

Reader: A reading from the *Apostolic Exhortation on Christian Joy*.

The joy of living in God's love begins here below. It is the joy of the kingdom of God. But it is granted on a steep road which requires a total confidence in the Father and in the Son, and a preference given to the kingdom. The message of Jesus promises joy above all, and it begins with the beatitudes.

Here ends the reading.   **Thanks be to God.**

Response: **Seek Ye First** or any suitable song.

Third Reading: Pope Paul VI, *Christian Joy*, May 9, 1975
[Mary experienced joy in her life.]

Reader: A reading from the *Apostolic Exhortation on Christian Joy*.

The Virgin Mary, accepting from Gabriel the announcement of Jesus' conception, manifested her joy before her cousin Elizabeth. She grasped, better than all other creatures, that God accomplishes wonderful things: his name is holy, he shows his mercy, he raises up the humble, he is faithful to his promises. Not that the apparent course of her life in any way departed from the ordinary, but she meditated on the least signs of God, pondering them in her heart. She was also open in an unlimited degree to the joy of the resurrection, and she was taken up, body and soul, into the glory of heaven. She is the perfect model of the Church both on earth and in glory.

Here ends the reading.   **Thanks be to God.**

Response: **Sing of Mary** or any suitable song.

Homily

Scriptural Litany of Joy

Minister: For the coming and presence of Jesus:

> **R.   Let us rejoice.**
>
> For the glad tidings announced at his birth: **R.**
>
> For Mary's exultant hymn of humility: **R.**
>
> For the Baptist, who leapt for joy in his mother's womb: **R.**
>
> For John's preaching of conversion and repentance: **R.**
>
> For the proclamation of the gospel: **R.**
>
> For the children who approached Jesus: **R.**
>
> For Zacchaeus in his conversion: **R.**
>
> For the hospitality of Martha, Mary and Lazarus: **R.**
>
> For the widow who gave from her poverty: **R.**
>
> For the miracles of Jesus: **R.**
>
> For his words of pardon: **R.**
>
> For salvation in and through Jesus: **R.**
>
> For all the signs of God's loving kindness: **R.**

Minister: With joy let us pray the prayer Jesus taught us.

All: **Our Father, . . .**

Concluding Rite

Blessing

Minister: May our prayer rise like incense in God's sight,
and may he receive it as a pleasing fragrance.

All: **Amen.**

Minister: May the Lord enkindle in us the fire of his love,
and the flame of everlasting charity.

All: **Amen.**

Minister: May the Father, the Son, and the Holy Spirit fill us with joy, and may we praise God with joyful hearts.

All: **Amen.**

Closing Song: **Rejoice, People Gathered This Day** or any suitable song.

A Father's Love—
Penitential Service

Introductory Rites

Opening Song: **To You, O Lord, I Lift My Soul** or any suitable song.

Call to Celebration

Minister: Those who are led by the Spirit of God are children of God.
You did not receive a spirit of slavery,
to fall back into fear,
but you received a spirit of adoption
through which we cry *Abba,* ''Father!''   Rom 8:14-15

All: **I have sinned against heaven . . .**
I no longer deserve to be called your child.   Lk 15:21

Minister: I tell you, in just the same way there will be more joy in heaven
over one sinner who repents
than over ninety-nine righteous people
who have no need of repentance.   Lk 15:7
If you forgive others their transgressions,
your heavenly Father will forgive you.   Mt 6:14

All: **Have mercy on me, O God, in your goodness.**   Ps 51:3

Reading of the Word of God

Gospel: Luke 15:11-32

[Celebrate the repentance and forgiveness of the sinner.]

*Two readers and the congregation may proclaim the gospel in dialogue to dramatize its
meaning.*

1:   A man had two sons, and the younger son said to his father,

All: **''Father, give me the share of the estate that should come to**
me.''

1:   So the father divided the property between them. After a few
days, the younger son collected all his belongings and set off to a
distant country where he squandered his inheritance on a life of

dissipation. When he had freely spent everything, a severe famine struck that country, and he found himself in dire need. So he hired himself out to one of the local citizens, who sent him to his farm to tend the swine. And he longed to eat his fill of the pods on which the swine fed, but nobody gave him any. Coming to his senses he thought,

All: **How many of my father's hired hands**
have more than enough food to eat,
but here I am, dying from hunger.
I shall get up and go to my father,
and I shall say to him,
"Father, I have sinned against heaven and against you.
I no longer deserve to be called your son;
treat me as you would one of your hired workers."

1: So he got up and went back to his father. While he was still a long way off, his father caught sight of him, and was filled with compassion. He ran to his son, embraced him and kissed him. His son said to him,

All: **"Father, I have sinned against heaven and against you;**
I no longer deserve to be called your son."

1: But the father said to his servants:

2: "Quickly bring the finest robe and put it on him; put a ring on his finger and sandals on his feet. Take the fattened calf and slaughter it. Then let us celebrate with a feast, because this son of mine was dead, and has come to life again; he was lost, and has been found."

1: Then the celebration began. Now the older son had been out in the field and, on his way back, as he neared the house, he heard the sound of music and dancing. He called one of the servants and asked what this might mean. The servant said to him,

2: "Your brother has returned and your father has slaughtered the fattened calf because he has him back safe and sound."

1: He became angry, and when he refused to enter the house, his father came out and pleaded with him. He said to his father in reply,

2: "Look, all these years I served you and not once did I disobey your orders; yet you never gave me even a young goat to feast on with my friends. But when your son returns who swallowed up your property with prostitutes, for him you slaughter the fattened calf."

1: He said to him,

2: "My son, you are here with me always; everything I have is yours. But now we must celebrate and rejoice, because your brother was dead and has come to life again; he was lost, and has been found.''

1:        This is the gospel of the Lord.

All: **Praise to you, Lord Jesus Christ.**

Response: **Yes, I Shall Arise** or any suitable song.

Homily

Resolution

(Wisdom 11:22-24)

All: **Before you, [Lord,] the whole universe is as a grain from a balance,**
          or a drop of morning dew come down upon the earth.
          But you have mercy on all, because you can do all things;
          and you overlook the sins of [all] that they may repent.
          For you love all things that are
          and loathe nothing that you have made;
          for what you hated, you would not have fashioned.

Concluding Rite

Minister: May mercy, peace and love be [ours]
            in abundance.   Jude 1:2

All: **Thanks be to God.**

Closing Song: **I Lift My Heart** or any suitable song.

FREEDOM—PENITENTIAL SERVICE

Introductory Rites

Opening Song: **Amazing Grace!** or any suitable song.

Call to Celebration

Minister: Gathered in the name of Jesus,
we prepare to open our hearts to the love of his Spirit,

All: **so that we may be inspired with more perfect love
of God and our neighbor.**

Opening Prayer

Minister: Let us pray.

All good God,
your Son freed us by his cross and resurrection.
In our frailty we have misused the gift of freedom.
We pray for deliverance from slavery to sin.
Help us to grow in the love of your commandments,
so that in obedience to your will
we may find our perfect freedom.

We ask this through Christ our Lord.

All: **Amen.**

Reading of the Word of God

First Reading: Vatican Council II, *The Church in the Modern World*, no. 17
[True freedom is the choice of what is good.]

Reader: A reading from the *Pastoral Constitution on the Church in the
Modern World*

Only in freedom can we direct ourselves toward goodness. Our
contemporaries make much of this freedom and pursue it eagerly;
and rightly so, to be sure. Often, however, they foster it perversely as
a license for doing whatever pleases them, even if it is evil.

For its part, authentic freedom is an exceptional sign of the
divine image within us. For God has willed that we be left ''subject to
our own free choice'' so that we can seek our Creator spontaneously,

and come freely to utter and blissful perfection through loyalty to Him. Hence our dignity demands that we act according to a knowing and free choice. Such a choice is personally motivated and prompted from within. It does not result from blind internal impulse nor from mere external pressure.

We achieve such dignity when, emancipating ourselves from all captivity to passion, we pursue our goal in a spontaneous choice of what is good, and procure for ourselves, through effective and skillful action, apt means to that end. Since our freedom has been damaged by sin, only by the help of God's grace can we bring such a relationship with God into full flower. Before the judgment seat of God each of us must render an account of our own life, whether we have done good or evil.

Here ends the reading. **Thanks be to God.**

Response: 1 Chronicles 16:11, 14, 10, 23, 35

All: **Look to the LORD in his strength;**
   seek to serve him constantly.
He, the LORD, is our God;
   throughout the earth his judgments prevail.
Glory in his holy name;
   rejoice, O hearts that seek the LORD!

Sing to the LORD, all the earth,
   announce his salvation, day after day.
And say, "Save us, O God, our savior,
   gather us and deliver us from the nations,
That we may give thanks to your holy name
   and glory in praising you."

Gospel: John 8:31-36
[The truth of Jesus' teaching sets us free.]

Response: **Make Us True Servants** or any suitable song.

Homily

Resolution

Psalm 32:1-2, 3-4, 5, 6-7, 10-11

   R.   Happy are those whose sins are forgiven.

Concluding Rite

Dismissal

Minister: You were called for freedom,
but do not use this freedom as an opportunity for the flesh;
rather serve one another through love.   Gal 5:13

All: **For freedom Christ set us free;
[we] stand firm and [will] not submit again
to the yoke of slavery.**   Gal 5:1

Closing Song: **You Fill the Day** or any suitable song.

OUR DAILY WORK—PENITENTIAL SERVICE

Introductory Rites

Opening Song: **Jesus, Our Divine Companion** or any suitable song.

Call to Celebration   (Psalm 145:8-10)

Minister: The LORD is gracious and merciful,

All: **slow to anger and of great kindness.**

Minister: The LORD is good to all

All: **and compassionate toward all his works.**

Minister: Let all your works give you thanks, O LORD,

All: **and let your faithful ones bless you.**

Penitential Rite

Minister: We take time away from the routine of our daily duties and responsibilities to gather as a community and reflect on our lives. As we look to the past, we see our weakness, negligence, failure and sin. As we live in the present, we rely on God's continuing mercy and assistance. As we resolve for the future, we are full of hope and promise.

All: **I confess to almighty God
             and to you, my brothers and sisters
             that I have sinned through my own fault.
             In my thoughts and in my words,
             in what I have done and in what I have failed to do.
             And I ask blessed Mary, ever-virgin,
             all the angels and saints,
             and you, my brothers and sisters,
             to pray for me to the Lord our God.**

Minister: May almighty God have mercy on us, forgive us our sins and bring us to everlasting life.

All: **Amen.**

Reading of the Word of God

First Reading: Colossians 3:14-15, 17, 23-24 (L559)
[Work for the Lord.]

Response: **All That I Am** or any suitable song.

Gospel: Luke 12:15-21 (L860-1)
[Grow rich in God's sight.]

Homily

Reflective Prayer

Minister: God worked to create this world
with its order, its beauty and its unexplored possibilities.
Let us thank him.

All: **Thank you, God, for the harmony of the seasons,**
the rhythm of sun and rain, seed time and harvest.
We look at the stars and marvel at what you have made.
We explore the surface of the moon and rejoice
in the amazing skills you give us and in your trust in us.
Thank you for believing in us
even when we mar your creation
and become arrogant with our powers.

Minister: Jesus Christ did the work of his Father,
bringing light into the darkness,
making our days holy by living in them to his Father's glory.

All: **Thank you, God, for Jesus' labors on our behalf.**
As he taught, healed and reconciled,
he became our example of the obedient Son.
Thank you for the ministry of reconciliation
which he entrusted to us, his people.

Silently consider Jesus' life and his invitation to each of us.

Minister: We enter into the labors of all who have gone before us.

All: **We praise you, God,**
for those who have made the world a better place to be.
For scholars and saints,

for sensitive people who loved their neighbor,
for pioneers who dared to go into the unknown,
for those who did quiet works of faith, hope and charity —
for all these we thank you.

Silently remember loved ones now deceased.

Minister: Praise God that he gives us strength to do our work.

All: **We are grateful for tasks that test our skills and use our talents.
We thank you for the sense of a job well done,
and for the challenges that will face us tomorrow.
We thank you for those who work with us.**

Silently thank God for particular co-workers.

Minister: Let us remember the many who serve us through their work.

All: **We acknowledge in gratitude parents, wives, husbands, and
those who hallow their work by helpfulness:
receptionists, secretaries, operators, clerks, custodians;
doctors, nurses, nurses' aides, surgeons, orderlies;
chaplains, pastors, educators, drivers, postal clerks;
police and fire fighters, mayors and delivery people.
Help them find joy in service.**

Silently recall others who serve with generosity.

Concluding Rite

Dismissal

Minister: May the Lord give us peace in our work.

All: **God, send us into our work with new resolves.
Help us to work out the problems that have perplexed us,
and to serve the people we meet.
May we see our work as part of your great plan
and find significance in what we do.
We do not know what any day will bring us,
but we do know the hour for serving you is always present.
We dedicate our hearts, minds and wills to your glory.**

Through Jesus Christ our Lord. Amen.

Closing Song: **Make Us True Servants** or any suitable song.

Our Call to Serve—
Penitential Service

Introductory Rites

Opening Song: **Here I Am, Lord** or any suitable song.

Call to Worship

Minister: The Lord God calls each of us to discipleship.
We are called to serve one another.
We are called to serve the church.

All: **The Spirit of the Lord is upon us.**
We are anointed to bring the Good News.   cf. Is 61:1

Opening Prayer

Minister: Let us pray.

God our Father,
in baptism you invited us to be your followers.
With your help may we daily understand more clearly
the challenge and joy of discipleship.
Let us be to one another
a constant reminder of the Spirit present among us.

We ask this through Christ our Lord.

All: **Amen.**

Reading of the Word of God

First Reading: 1 Samuel 3:1-10; 19-20 (L307-2)
   [The Lord calls Samuel.]

Response: Psalm 25:4-7; 20-21
   R. To you, O Lord, I lift my soul.

Gospel: Matthew 3:13-17 (L21-A)
   [The Father calls Jesus and proclaims him his beloved Son.]

Homily

Resolution

Minister: The call of the Lord is a personal call.
He calls us to life, to service, to conversion.
Come, let us return to the Lord; he will heal us.
He will revive us after two days;
on the third day he will raise us up.

**R. We are the children of the Father.
His forgiveness and favor rest on us.**

Return to the LORD, your God,
for gracious and merciful is he. **R.**   Jl 2:13

No one can enter the kingdom of God
without being begotten of water and the Spirit. **R.**   Jn 3:5

Unless you turn and become like little children,
you will not enter the kingdom of heaven. **R.**   Mt 8:12

Concluding Rite

Dismissal

Minister: I urge you
to live in a manner worthy of the call you have received,
with all humility and gentleness, with patience,
bearing with one another through love,
striving to preserve the unity of the
spirit through the bond of peace: Eph 4:1-3

All: **one body and one Spirit,
as [we] were also called to the one hope of [our] call;
one Lord, one faith, one baptism;
one God and Father of all,
who is over all and through all and in all.**   Eph 4:4-5

Minister: The LORD bless you and keep you!
The LORD let his face shine upon you,
and be gracious to you!
The LORD look upon you kindly
and give you peace!   Nm 6:24-26

All: **Amen.**

Minister: Let us go in peace to follow Jesus' call.

All: **Thanks be to God.**

Closing Song: **Make Us True Servants** or any suitable song.

THANKSGIVING—PENITENTIAL SERVICE

Introductory Rites

Opening Song: **We Gather Together** or any suitable song.

Call to Celebration

Minister: Give thanks to the Father, who has made you fit to share in the
inheritance of the holy ones in light.   Col 1:12

All: **He delivered us from the power of darkness
and transferred us to the kingdom of his beloved Son, in whom
we have redemption,
the forgiveness of sins.**   Col 1:13-14

Opening Prayer

Minister: Let us pray.

Merciful Lord,
pardon your people their offenses
and through your bountiful goodness
free us from the sins we have committed in our frailty.

We ask this through Christ our Lord.

All: **Amen.**

Reading of the Word of God

First Reading: Ephesians 1:3-10 (L913-2)
[Our redemption through Christ's blood is God's favor to us.]

Response: Psalm 103:1-2, 3-4, 8-9 (L345)
R.   The Lord is kind and merciful.

Gospel: Luke 17:11-19 (L885-2)
[Gratitude is due God's favor.]

Homily

Litany

Minister: With sorrow for taking
God's goodness and loving kindness for granted,
we pray to the Lord:

R.   Lord have mercy.

With sorrow for refusing to love as we are commanded,
we pray to the Lord: **R.**

With sorrow for misusing and abusing
the beauty and resources of the earth,
we pray to the Lord: **R.**

With sorrow for neglecting to respond
to God's inspiration and grace,
we pray to the Lord: **R.**

With sorrow for refusing to respond to those in need,
we pray to the Lord: **R.**

With sorrow for omitting to give thanks
every day of our lives,
we pray to the Lord: **R.**

With sorrow for our ingratitude,
manifested by our deliberate sins,
we pray to the Lord: **R.**

Concluding Rite

(Te Deum)

All: **You are God: we praise you;**
You are the Lord: we acclaim you;
You are the eternal Father:
All creation worships you.
To you all angels, all the powers of heaven,
Cherubim and Seraphim, sing in endless praise:
    Holy, holy, holy Lord, God of power and might,
    heaven and earth are full of your glory.
The glorious company of apostles praise you.
The noble fellowship of prophets praise you.
The white-robed army of martyrs praise you.
Throughout the world the holy Church acclaims you:
    Father, of majesty unbounded,
    your true and only Son, worthy of all worship,
    and the Holy Spirit, advocate and guide.

You, Christ are the king of glory,
eternal Son of the Father.
When you became human to set us free
you did not spurn the Virgin's womb.
You overcame the sting of death,
and opened the kingdom of heaven to all believers.
You are seated at God's right hand in glory.
We believe that you will come, and be our judge.
Come then, Lord, sustain your people,
bought with the price of your own blood,
and bring us with your saints
to glory everlasting.

Closing Song: **Now Thank We All Our God** or any suitable song.

Services compiled by:

Rev. Jerome S. Siwek and James E. Wilbur
> A Vigil Service Before Christmas

Rev. Jerome S. Siwek, James E. Wilbur and Rev. Medard P. Laz
> Independence Day Celebration

Rev. Jerome S. Siwek
> Advent Vespers
> Advent Penitential Service
> Lenten Preparation—Home or School
> Lenten Vespers
> Lent's Meaning—Penitential Service
> Joy at Easter—Prayer Service
> Hope—Penitential Service
> Home Service for Pentecost
> Spirit of Joy—Prayer Service
> Respect for Life—Penitential Service
> Christian Joy—Penitential Service
> A Father's Love—Penitential Service
> Freedom—Penitential Service
> Our Daily Work—Penitential Service

Rev. Joseph D. Slater, S.T.L.
> Light in the Lord—Penitential Service
> Scripture Service for Epiphany
> Now Is the Acceptable Time—Penitential Service
> Pentecost—Season for Renewal
> Jesus in Glory—Penitential Service
> Heart for Hearts—Penitential Service

Madeline L. Brock
> Lenten Meal—Home Service
> A Lenten Service Based on the Final Words of Christ
> Prayers for a Parish Meeting
> Home Service—The Christian Family
> Service for Christian Unity
> The Gift of Beauty in the Land—Scripture Service

James E. Wilbur

> In the Spirit—Scripture Service
> Service for the Opening of School
> Service for Travel
> Home Service for Shut-Ins

Madeline L. Brock and James E. Wilbur

> Service to Close the School Year
> Picnic Service
> Prayer Service Before Elections

Sr. Roseann Kasyaka, OSF, The National Vocation Council

> Our Call to Serve—Penitential Service

Rev. James J. Close and James E. Wilbur

> Intercessions for Holy Family Day

Rev. Medard P. Laz and James E. Wilbur

> Behold Your Mother—May Crowning Service

Rev. Medard P. Laz

> A New Beginning—Penitential Service